THE
SPLICING
HANDBOOK
SECOND EDITION

THE
SPLICING
HANDBOOK

SECOND EDITION

Techniques for
Modern and Traditional Ropes

Barbara Merry
with John Darwin

ADLARD COLES NAUTICAL
London

Published by Adlard Coles Nautical
an imprint of A & C Black Publishers Ltd
37 Soho Square, London WID 3QZ
www.adlardcoles.com

Copyright © International Marine 1987, 2000

First edition published 1987 by Nautical Books
Second edition published 2000 by Adlard Coles Nautical
Reprinted 2003

ISBN 0-7136-6846-6

A CIP catalogue record for this book is available from the British Library.

NOTE: While all reasonable care has been taken in the publication of this book,
the publisher takes no responsibility for the use of the methods or products
described in the book.

CONTENTS

ACKNOWLEDGMENTS

Thanks to Dave and Mike at T.W.E. Company.

THE SPLICING HANDBOOK

SECOND EDITION

ONE

INTRODUCTION TO SPLICING

Rope in use is attached to something else—to another rope, to an object to be moved or prevented from moving, or to an object that prevents the rope from moving. The attachment can be accomplished with a knot, but knots are bulky and, by their nature, cut the breaking strength of the rope in half. The alternative is a splice, which is capable of attaining a rope's full strength.

Splicing teaches you not only about the splice itself, but also about the construction and quality of the raw material. The knowledge gained from practicing the splices in this handbook should enable you to splice *any* general-purpose rope. But remember the wise advice, as true today as it ever has been: "Measure twice, cut once."

No single splicing technique can work on all rope because the constructions vary considerably. Rope designers, who are functional artists much like architects, seek a perfect construction using the characteristics of various fibers: strengths, abrasion resistance, weight, shrinkage, and elasticity. They must consider resistance to heat, cold, sunlight, chemicals, water, dye, and microorganisms, as well as construction possibilities such as braiding, twisting, knitting, plaiting, wrapping, and gluing.

ROPE CONSTRUCTION

Egyptians on the Mediterranean worked with twisted and braided ropes 3,000 years ago, as did seamen 12,000 miles away in Asia. Their ropes, knots, and splices were much like those we use today, except that ropes of strong synthetic fibers have all but replaced plant fibers over the past few decades. With increased international shipping, ropes from all over the world are now evident in large commercial harbors.

Any rope is a bundle of textile fibers combined in a usable form. For example, a ½-inch-diameter (12 mm) nylon rope might have 90,000 tiny fibers, each with a tensile strength of 2 ounces (56.7 g), giving it a potential breaking strength of 11,000 pounds (4,950 kg) if the fibers could be pulled in such a way that each achieved its maximum strength. The 90,000 fibers can be bonded, twisted (laid), or braided, or these construction techniques can be combined in one rope. Regardless of the construction, the actual breaking strength of the finished rope will be less than the potential strength of its aggregate fibers due to a shearing action on the twisted fibers when the rope is loaded. This effect is most extreme in laid rope: the U.S. standard for ½-inch (12 mm) three-strand nylon rope, for example, is a breaking strength of 5,800 pounds (2,610 kg); for ½-inch nylon double-braid, it's 15 percent higher.

The old standby, three-strand twisted nylon rope, is the most economical rope available today, at about half the cost of double-braided nylon. It consists of fibers (often nylon, but sometimes polyester, polypropylene, aramid, or polyethylene) spun into yarns, which are then formed into the strands. Nylon three-strand is commonly used for anchor rodes and mooring and docking lines— applications where its strength, pronounced stretchiness, resistance to chafe, and reasonable cost are all appreciated.

Double-braid rope came into use with the discovery that careful design and construction could induce a braided core to share a load equally with its braided cover. When you work with this rope, you must preserve the original coat-to-core spatial relationship to retain its inherent strength, so tie the Slip Knot—called for in the splice directions for this construction—both properly and tightly.

Dacron double-braid is stronger than three-strand twisted nylon rope (or three-strand or single-braid Dacron, for that matter), but it is also nearly double the price for ½-inch (12 mm) rope, and the difference in cost should be considered against the line's intended use. (Dacron is a DuPont trade name for polyester, and the two terms are often used interchangeably.) Whenever the breaking strength of a rope is critical, the manufacturer's specifications should be consulted. Some low-cost rope on the market is made to look like double-braid, but it is not, so check the product carefully and deal with reputable suppliers.

Polyester double-braid rope is low-stretch and resists kinking and hockling; it handles well and is good for halyards and sheets.

Single-braid (also known as solid-braid) polyester is more supple, less expensive, stretchier, and somewhat less strong and durable than double-braid. It's useful for multipart mainsheets or vangs where ease of handling is prized and minimizing stretch matters less than it does for, say, jibsheets.

Braid with three-strand core is another common rope for running rigging on yachts. As its name implies, the outer cover is braided, in this case with 16 plaits or braids. The core, a three-strand twist, carries most of the strength. Often called Marlow, for its English manufacturer, it is sold with standard and fuzzy covers, the latter being soft on the hands and holding knots well. The covers are available in colors—a convenience when, for example, one must find a halyard quickly in a maze of running rigging. Marlow can be difficult to find in some areas.

Dacron braid with a Dacron parallel-fiber core is another rope with most of the strength in the core. It stretches much less than double-braid and, pound for pound, it is as strong as stainless steel wire (see Wire Halyard Replacement Chart), so there is a trend toward using it to replace wire on recreational nonracing sailboats. In the United States, Sta-Set X (New England Ropes) is a popular brand. This rope is also stiff and a poor choice where bend and flex are important, such as when a line must pass through a block.

Wire Halyard Replacement Chart, in. (mm)		
7 × 19 Stainless Wire	Braid with Parallel Core Sta-Set X	Double Braid Samson XLS 900
⅛ (3)	³⁄₁₆ (5)	⁵⁄₁₆ (7)
⁵⁄₃₂ (4)	¼ (6)	⅜ (9)
³⁄₁₆ (5)	⁵⁄₁₆ (7)	⁷⁄₁₆ (11)
⁷⁄₃₂ (6)	⁵⁄₁₆ (7)	½ (12)
¼ (6)	⅜ (9)	⁹⁄₁₆ (21)

This chart is for general comparison only. Follow the manufacturer's specific recommendations for all working loads.

Hollow-braid rope of polypropylene floats and is most often used for water-ski towlines and around life rings.

Nylon eight-plait rope, also called square braid, is common on commercial vessels. It consists of four-strand pairs, one member of each pair having right-laid yarns and the other having left-laid yarns. (To determine the direction of the lay, consider the rope with its end pointing away from you. Right-lay spirals up and to the right.)

More rounded than eight-plait, twelve-plait rope is used most often for towing hawsers. The plaited ropes are easy to inspect for damage and can be dropped in a heap on deck without hockling.

Inexpensive rope such as clothesline, often sold precoiled in hardware stores, is not suitable for marine use.

SYNTHETIC ROPE MATERIALS

Once there were only ropes made from plant fibers such as flax, hemp, jute, sisal, cotton, and later, manila. Then there were the popular synthetics: nylon, polyester (Dacron), and polypropylene. Now, from research labs around the world, new higher-strength rope fibers with more names than can easily be remembered are available for discriminating rope users. Spectra, Dyneema, Kevlar,

Danline, Cerfilene, EuroSteel, Iceline, Certran, copolymer, Zylon, aramid, and high-modulus polyethylene fiber—the choices can bewilder mariners, and the names are often misused and misunderstood. We will tell a few tales about some of the more popular rope fibers so that you old salts can converse with the technocrats of the rope world.

Dyneema is the trade name used in Europe by a Netherlandish company called DSM for a very high-strength, high-modulus polyethylene fiber. In the United States, this product is sold under the trademark Spectra (Allied Signal Company). Until the advent of this polyethylene fiber with extremely high molecular orientation, the only rope fiber stronger than nylon was Kevlar (DuPont), an aramid fiber.

Both Kevlar and Spectra ropes are at least twice the strength of equal-diameter nylon rope, and they have hardly any stretch. Kevlar is ten times as strong as steel, pound for pound, and Spectra is six times as strong as steel. These ropes would be everywhere if they didn't cost six times as much as nylon or Dacron. Despite the high prices, however, Spectra and Kevlar have become standard choices for many jobs. Both are commonly available in doublebraid and eight-plait constructions.

One of the first uses of Kevlar rope was in a U.S. Navy floating dry dock, where it enabled line handlers using no power to maneuver ships precisely as they entered the dock. This job had previously required heavy steel wire and power winches.

Today, the largest tankers use docklines of Kevlar and Spectra, having found that the high initial cost is quickly recouped by savings from fewer injury claims by crew members and docking personnel handling the lighter lines. Kevlar rope has three main disadvantages for recreational boaters: it's expensive, it's stiff and hard to handle (though less so than wire rope), and it lacks durability because of internal abrasion.

Kevlar is distinguished by its fine texture and soft gold color. An open flame will not melt or burn Kevlar ropes, although the bitter end will char slightly, and threadlike Kevlar yarns will turn bright red and leave a charcoal ash. The only other rope fibers that don't melt or burn are Nomex (DuPont), which is not high-strength, and a Japanese fiber, Zylon, which is even stronger than Kevlar. Zylon is seldom seen in rope form, however. Kevlar and Zylon are both heavy, dense fibers that readily sink in either freshwater or salt water.

Large fishing trawlers have replaced their wire-rope tackles and whips with braided Spectra line. Spectra seems to last forever, while the steel-wire rope would last only a month lifting heavy nets full of fish many times a day.

Spectra and Dyneema both float in water, yet another major factor in their use as tugboat bow and stern lines. You can melt these high-tech polyethylenes with a soldering gun or an open flame. They burn in the presence of a flame but self-extinguish when the flame is removed. Spectra and Dyneema come in many colors, but white and shades of gray are most common. Strong, durable, supple, soft to the touch, low-stretch, and easier to handle than Kevlar or Sta-Set X, Spectra is finding increasing favor as halyards on spare-no-expense sailboats.

Right now, the most promising new rope fibers are the copolymers, which are chemical mixtures primarily of polyethylene and polypropylene. Organic chemists have teamed up with textile engineers to invent these extremely strong and durable rope fibers, and rope manufacturers around the world now have extruders turning out light, strong, low-stretch copolymer fibers that make a supple rope at a very reasonable price. Copolymer is much stronger, easier to handle, and only a little more expensive than polypropylene, and it will likely make polypropylene rope obsolete within a short time.

One of the earliest uses of copolymer was in the New England lobster-fishing industry. Lobster fishermen use a tremendous amount of rope with their traps, and it would be hard to find anyone who knows rope better than one who makes his or her living handling pot warps every day. Prior to 1950, these ropes were sisal and manila. With the advent of synthetics, polypropylene became the fiber of choice because it was cheap, it floated, and it didn't rot. Everyone on the coast of New England remembers these colorful ropes washing up on beaches everywhere, the predominant yellow becoming a symbol of the lobster industry. But recently, copolymers have almost wholly supplanted polypropylene. Copolymer fibers are so good that even poorly made rope works well. These fibers will soon be everywhere in braided and twisted ropes. Leading brands include Cerfilene, Steelline, and EuroSteel.

As if all these new rope materials and constructions weren't enough, yet another innovation is becoming increasingly popular of late: rope coatings. A coating of urethane is available in a variety of colors and can be applied over various synthetics. The coating is tough and durable, considerably reduces abrasion, and practically eliminates snagging.

SUMMARY OF ROPE CHARACTERISTICS

Both the materials and the construction of synthetic ropes mandate splicing techniques that were never needed with natural fibers. For example, manila, a natural fiber, holds its shape after it has been unlaid, but nylon changes shape very quickly as the strands slip away from each other and divide into yarns. The splicer must adapt to this tendency by sealing the rope ends as described in the rest of this book.

Synthetics present a range of characteristics (see General Characteristics of Synthetic Marine Rope Materials, next page). Manila, once used almost exclusively, is now favored mainly by traditionalists. It is heavy for its strength—twice the weight of nylon—and rots from the inside, a problem that is difficult to detect.

General Characteristics of Synthetic Marine Rope Materials

Material	Strength	Stretch	Shrinkage	Flotation	Cost	Common Uses
Nylon	strong	stretches	shrinks	sinks	moderate	mooring lines and docklines
Polyester (Dacron)	strong	low-stretch	low-shrink	sinks	moderate	sheets and halyards
Polypropylene	low-strength	low-stretch	low-shrink	floats	economical	water-ski towlines
Aramid (Kevlar)	very strong	low-stretch	no-shrink	sinks	high	running rigging
High-Tenacity Copolymers	strong	low-stretch	low-shrink	floats	economical	sheets and tackles
High-Tenacity Polyethylene (Spectra and Dyneema)	very strong	low-stretch	no-shrink	floats	high	running rigging

Polypropylene is the lightest synthetic rope now in production. Its great advantage is its ability to float on fresh and salt water. It has a low melting point and should not be used near heat-producing mechanical devices. It also has a low resistance to sunlight.

Ropes made of nylon are strong, but stretch significantly. They have excellent resistance to sunlight, common alkalis, and acids. Polyester (Dacron and Terylene) is a low-stretch rope with a low tensile strength. Both nylon and polyester are sold in spun and filament form. The spun rope is usually fuzzy and is made of fibers 4 to 10 inches (100 to 254 mm) long; the continuous-filament rope has a shiny surface and is stronger and heavier.

Quick Guide to Strength of Rope Materials

Diameter in Inches of Three-Strand or Double-Braid Nylon Rope

	$\frac{1}{16}$	$\frac{1}{8}$	$\frac{3}{16}$	$\frac{1}{4}$	$\frac{5}{16}$	$\frac{3}{8}$	$\frac{7}{16}$	$\frac{1}{2}$	$\frac{5}{8}$	$\frac{3}{4}$	$\frac{7}{8}$	1
Diameter in millimeters	1.5	3	5	6	8	9	11	12	16	19	22	25
Braid size	2	4	6	8	10	12	14	16	20	24	28	32
Circumference in inches	$\frac{3}{16}$	$\frac{3}{8}$	$\frac{5}{8}$	$\frac{3}{4}$	1	$1\frac{1}{8}$	$1\frac{1}{4}$	$1\frac{1}{2}$	2	$2\frac{1}{4}$	$2\frac{3}{4}$	3
Weight in feet per pound (kg)	400 (268	200 134	100 67	65 44	40 27	30 20	20 13.4	16 10.7	10 6.7	7 4.7	5 3.4	4 2.7)
Breaking strength in pounds (kg)	200 (90	400 180	750 337.5	1,000 450	2,000 900	3,000 1,350	4,000 1,800	6,000 2,700	10,000 4,500	17,000 7,650	20,000 9,000	25,000 11,250)

Aramid (Kevlar)—40 percent heavier than nylon; more than 200 percent stronger
Copolymers—20 percent lighter than nylon; about the same strength
Polyester—20 percent heavier than nylon; about the same strength
Polyethylene (Spectra and Dyneema)—20 percent lighter than nylon; 200 percent stronger
Polypropylene—20 percent lighter in weight than nylon; 20 percent weaker

Note: This chart is for three-strand and double braid rope of the same weight and quality. The safe working load of rope is about 10 percent of its breaking strength. In *all* critical situations, consult the manufacturer's local recommendations.

Combination rope is any rope constructed of more than one synthetic fiber. Most common on fishing boats is three-strand twisted polyester and polypropylene, which has the general characteristics of 100 percent polyester but is cheaper.

Kevlar, DuPont's aramid fiber, is combined with Dacron for extra strength in some double-braid ropes.

SMALL STUFF

Small stuff is cordage of less than $\frac{3}{16}$-inch (5 mm) (to the recreational boater) or $\frac{1}{2}$-inch (12 mm) (to the commercial mariner) diameter. When constructed of firm, spliceable manila or nylon, it is favored by the boatowner for light-duty use and decorative projects.

Definitions within the rope industry differ, however, and some also group the following with small stuff!

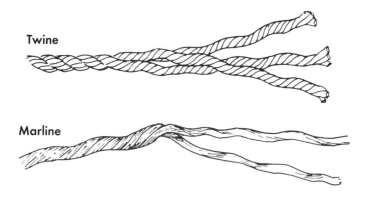

- **Twine** doesn't look like rope, although it is composed of fibers. It is usually less than $3/16$ inch (5 mm) in diameter. Waxed whipping twine is constructed of nylon or polyester and coated with wax to make whipping and seizing easier. The wax also protects against weathering.
- **Marline** consists of two strands of hemp, left-laid, and is coated with tar to protect against weathering, giving it a characteristic burned odor. It can be used for lashing or seizing.

ROPE CARE

It's foolish to buy good rope and then treat it carelessly because rope that is damaged will have a reduced breaking strength and a shorter life. Here are some ways to preserve the lifespan of your rope:

- To take rope off a storage reel properly, avoiding kinks, twists, or hockles in the line, let the reel rotate freely around a horizontal pipe suspended or supported at both ends.
- Store rope in a clean, dry area, off the floor, out of sunlight, and away from acid fumes.
- Keep rope from chafing against standing rigging and rough surfaces. Be wary of rusty or sharp chocks, bitts, and winches that will abrade the rope. Pulleys and blocks should be correctly sized and should turn freely.

- If a rope is chafed or frayed, cut out the damaged portion and splice. A good splice is safer than a damaged section.
- It is not generally necessary to oil or lubricate rope; if you do, use a product that is specifically designed for that purpose.
- Use whipping, tape, or an end splice on the bitter end of the rope to prevent unlaying.
- Check rope often for deterioration, opening the lay of three-strand and plaited rope for inspection.
- If rope is dragged over the ground, rocks and dirt can be picked up. Eventually, these particles can work into the rope, cutting the fibers.
- The proper way to dry a line is to lay it up on a grating in long fakes to allow good air circulation, thus preventing mildew and rot.
- Don't hesitate to wash synthetic rope by hand. Coil and tie it loosely, wash with a mild soap, then lay it out to dry.
- Don't use a rope in a situation where strength is critical if the rope has ever been subjected to a sudden, heavy load.
- A smooth taper will result in a more efficient splice.

SPLICING TOOLS

It's part of the splicing tradition to use tools that aid in separating the strands of rope. Just as high-tech rope and synthetic materials require new splicing techniques, they also mandate specialized tools to facilitate those procedures.

The Swedish fid is used for three-strand, eight-plait, and twelve-plait rope. The pointed end separates tightly twisted strands, and the concave blade allows individual strands to be pulled into position. It is easiest to work with a fid that is in proportion to the diameter of the rope, but any fid that is not too small to guide the rope will do. Swedish fids increase in circumference with length and are available in lengths of 6 inches for about $4.50, 12 inches for $6.50, and 14 inches (150, 300, and 350 mm) for $7.50 (these prices are

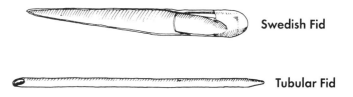

Swedish Fid

Tubular Fid

approximates for shore areas; if you're inland, prices are probably higher).

Tubular fids aid in splicing double-braid rope, which consists of a hollow braided core surrounded by a braided cover. When the core is removed from the cover during splicing, the cover becomes a hollow tube. The tubular fid, also called a Samson fid, guides the rope through these passageways as the splice is worked.

The fid has a pointed end to ease movement through the rope and an indented end where the working end of the rope is inserted. It is important that this be a snug fit, so the fids are made in sizes corresponding to standard rope diameters. If you have on hand a fid that is only slightly too large, the rope can be held in place with tape.

Measurements taken on the rope during splicing commonly use portions of the appropriate fid's length as units. A full fid length is the entire length of the fid; short and long fid lengths are marked on the fid. (See Approximate Lengths of Fid Sections table.) Tubular fids range in price from about $4.25 for the ¼-inch-diameter (6 mm) to $6.00 for ⅝-inch (16 mm).

Approximate Lengths of Fid Sections, in. (mm)			
Rope Diameter	Short	Long	Full
¼ (6)	2 (51)	3½ (89)	5½ (140)
⁵⁄₁₆ (8)	2½ (64)	4¼ (108)	6¾ (171)
⅜ (9)	3 (76)	4¾ (120)	7¾ (197)
⁷⁄₁₆ (11)	3½ (89)	6 (152)	9½ (241)
½ (12)	4 (101)	7 (178)	11 (279)
⁹⁄₁₆ (14)	4¼ (108)	8 (203)	12¼ (311)
⅝ (16)	4½ (114)	9½ (241)	14 (356)

A special splicing tool sold by Marlow Ropes, manufacturer of braid with three-strand core, is necessary to splice that rope. The tool is usually available where the rope is sold and consists of a small-diameter wire with a hook at one end and an eye at the other. The hook is used as a handle; the eye, threaded with one or more of the core strands, is pulled behind.

Splicing Tool

A Uni-Fid (New England Ropes, Fall River, Massachusetts) is needed to splice braid with parallel core. This rope has a core of parallel fibers wrapped in a gauze-like material, all within a braided cover. The tool consists of a small-diameter wire with a hook smaller than that on the Marlow splicing tool. A pointed end on the Uni-Fid is pushed through the rope, while the hook, which has been inserted through the gauze, follows behind.

Uni-Fid

The Uni-Fid, like the tubular fid, is divided into fid lengths, and the table comparing fid lengths to inches applies equally to it.

The venerable marlinspike shown here will easily splice wire $1/2$ to $3/4$ inch in diameter. A marlinspike is usually made of steel with a tip tapered like a duck's bill. This tool comes in a variety of sizes; I've seen them from 3 inches to 5 feet (75 mm to 1.5 m).

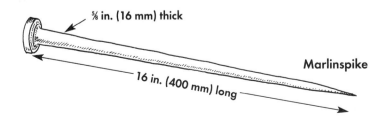

⅝ in. (16 mm) thick

Marlinspike

16 in. (400 mm) long

The two needlelike tools here are helpful when splicing some of the smaller sizes of "braided" ropes. These two implements are special favorites of mine. The long, thin needle with the eye is called a *sacking needle*. It's an ideal tool for pulling rope strands into place or rope cores into, out from, or down coat centers. The other tool (I've forgotten where I found it) was the tool of choice when John Darwin and I developed the copolymer splice. Ropes are classified as textiles, so any tool or instrument associated with any kind of sewing is of possible use to the rigger, knot-tier, or splicer. For instance, a stainless steel set of forceps is a most helpful alternative to needle-nose pliers when it's necessary to dive into the center of a fancy knot or tiny splice.

Sacking Needle

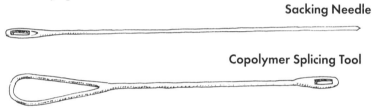

Copolymer Splicing Tool

These needles "knit" fishing nets and, like their cousin the weaver's shuttle, they hold and dispense cordage to grow the cloth. The needles come in different sizes to assist in making different sized mesh.

When applying seizing, short sections of service (chafe gear), or applying service to smaller sized ropes or wires, these needles are very helpful. They hold a lot of cordage and provide a comfortable grip while applying the twine under tension.

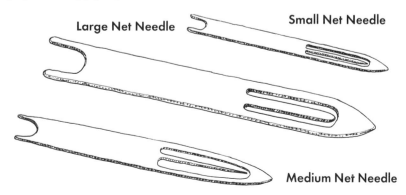

Large Net Needle

Small Net Needle

Medium Net Needle

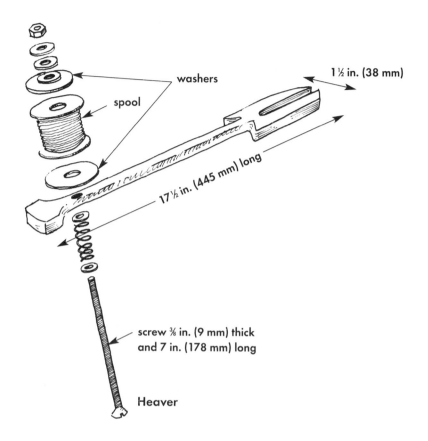

washers

spool

1 ½ in. (38 mm)

17 ½ in. (445 mm) long

screw ⅜ in. (9 mm) thick
and 7 in. (178 mm) long

Heaver

A handmade serving tool, the *heaver* is the arborist answer to the sailor's serving mallet. This tool is easy to master and easy to make. Any hardware store can supply the hardware. Use a band saw to shape the body and fashion the fork end. Drill the hole for the screw, then sand, stain, and varnish.

Not all splicing tools are used to manipulate rope during the working of a splice. The thimble is such a tool; it is a teardrop-shaped metal support for an Eye Splice, with a grooved outer edge for the rope.

Variations of the Eye Splice are found throughout this handbook, showing its popularity and virtuosity despite differences in rope construction and materials. Without a thimble, it is effective for light-duty use, such as on a topping lift or dinghy painter. With a thimble, the Eye Splice is ready for heavy use, when wear and chafe must be considered. A thimble should be used whenever the line will be attached to chain, swivels, or shackles, such as on the anchor end of an anchor rode.

Thimbles are available in only one eye size for any given diameter of rope. If a larger eye is needed for light-duty use and some protection is desired, service can be placed over the crown of the eye to substitute for a thimble.

Thimble

If you can't locate any of these tools locally, you can order them from me at The Marlinspike Artist, 360-C Gooseberry Road, Wakefield, Rhode Island 02879, U.S.A., 401-783-5404.

TWO

THREE-STRAND TWISTED ROPE

Technique is important to preserve splice strength, even with basic three-strand rope, which is sold in sizes ranging from $\frac{1}{8}$ to 2 inches (3 to 50 mm) in diameter.

EYE SPLICE

This is the most common splice. Take care that the tucks lie neatly, and that you complete at least three or four rounds of tucks (the Cordage Institute recommends a minimum of four rounds of tucks for all splices in three-strand).

TOOLS AND MATERIALS

Three-strand twisted rope
Swedish fid
Vinyl tape or whipping twine
Scissors or sharp knife
Hot knife or heat source
Ruler
Thimble (optional)

Unlay (i.e., untwist) the rope for 2 or 3 inches (50 to 80 mm) and tape each of the three individual ends or seize them tightly with twine (see chapter 13). Tape again at the point where the unlaying should end; for this splice in ³/₄-inch (19 mm) rope, that would be about 16 inches (400 mm) from the working end for four tucks. Add the amount of rope necessary to form the eye, or loop. Tape again. This spot is called the *throat* of the splice (see next page).

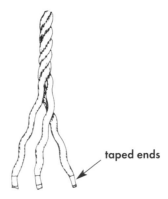

taped ends

Unlay back to the first piece of tape. To avoid a twist in the eye of the finished splice, untwist the rope just half a turn between the pieces of tape.

To do the first tuck, raise a strand just below the tape on the standing part of the rope and insert the middle working strand under it. You can usually do this with your fingers, but if the rope is twisted too tightly, use a Swedish fid (see page 12). Insert this splicing tool under the strand, and then place the middle working strand through the fid. Pull the strand into place and remove the tool.

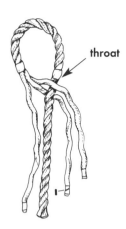

throat

The first time you work the splice, place a single hash mark on the strand that you just tucked. Numbering the working strands should help you to keep track of the tucking process.

Tuck the next working strand over the strand you just tucked under, and under the strand just below it. Mark this with two hash marks.

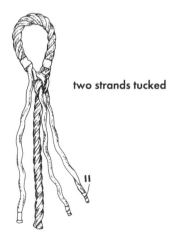

two strands tucked

Turn the entire piece over. You have one working strand left to tuck, and there is one strand left in the standing part of the rope that doesn't have a working strand under it. Make this tuck, continuing to work counter to the lay, or twist, of the rope (left to right in the drawings). Mark with three hash marks.

The first round of tucks is now complete. Tighten if necessary by pulling on the strand ends.

Take care when you tuck that you use all three strands in each round, and that you tuck under a strand in the standing part of the rope and not under one of your working strands.

Make three more rounds of tucks unless the rope is nylon, which holds better with five or six rounds.

For a smooth, better-looking splice, finish with the California method: After the rounds of tucks are complete, the first strand is left as is. The next strand is tucked once (as in the beginning steps) and the last strand is tucked twice.

Cut the ends off close, seal or melt the ends of synthetic rope with a hot knife or match, and remove the tape.

DECORATIVE EYE SPLICE

The decorative knot set at the neck of this dressed-up version of the Eye Splice does not affect its strength, but you should position the knot to avoid chafing when the splice is in use.

TOOLS AND MATERIALS

Three-strand twisted rope
Swedish fid
Vinyl tape or whipping twine
Scissors or sharp knife
Hot knife or heat source
Ruler

Unlay (untwist) the rope for 2 or 3 inches (50 to 80 mm), and tape each of the individual ends or seize them tightly with twine (see chapter 13). Tape again at the point where the unlaying should end. For this splice in ³/₄-inch (19 mm) rope, that would be 24 inches (0.6 m) from the working end of the rope. Add the amount of rope necessary to form the eye and tape again at the throat of the splice.

Unlay the rope back to the first piece of tape. To avoid a twist in the eye of the finished splice, untwist the rope just a half turn between the pieces of tape.

To do the first tuck, raise a strand just below the tape on the standing part of the rope and insert the middle working strand under it. You can usually do this with your fingers, but if the line is twisted too tightly, use a Swedish fid.

Tuck the next working strand over the strand you just tucked under, and under the strand just below it.

Turn the entire piece over. You have one working strand left to tuck, and there is one strand in the standing part of the rope that doesn't have a working strand under it. Make this tuck, continuing to work counter to the lay of the rope (left to right in the drawings).

Take care when you are tucking that you use all three strands in each round, and that you tuck under a strand in the standing part of the rope and not under one of your working strands.

The first round of tucks is now complete; tighten by pulling on the strand ends. To this point, the procedure is identical to that for the basic Eye Splice.

Now tie a Double Wall and Crown Knot as follows. Hold the throat of the splice between your thumb and forefinger with the strands emerging upward and spreading over the top of your fist, like the petals of a flower. To begin the wall knot, the first step in this three-step knot, take any strand and, moving counterclockwise, lead it over the strand next to it. (We will call this the *second strand*.) Allow the bight (loop) formed to remain prominent because you will need it later.

The second strand leads under the first strand, then under the third strand, as in the drawing. The third strand then leads under the second strand and up through the bight formed in the first step. This sounds complicated, but if you follow the illustration as you work, you'll see it is straightforward.

Gather the knot evenly, but keep it loose.

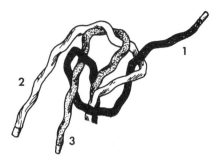

Take any strand and, continuing to work counterclockwise, lead it over the strand next to it, leaving a bight. Lead the second strand over the first strand, then over the third strand. Lead the third strand over the second strand and down through the bight.

The third and final step doubles the entire knot; this is the simplest part of the entire process. Beginning with any strand, duplicate its journey through the knot by eyeballing, poking, and wiggling it. (You left the knot loose in anticipation of this step.)

The strand's journey began near the point where its end now emerges. Guide the end back into the knot at that point and re-trace the circuit—in effect, doubling the strand. Take care as you work that you don't separate other parallel pairs. It's so easy once you get rolling that you have only to stop yourself from going too far. If the strand starts to appear in triplicate, you need to back up a little. Repeat this process for all three strands, and you'll have doubled the knot. Now cinch the strands firmly and evenly.

For a smooth, better-looking splice, finish with the California method: After three full rounds of tucks (five with nylon rope), the first strand is left as is. The next strand is tucked once (as in the beginning steps) and the last strand is tucked twice.

Cut the ends off close, seal or melt the ends of synthetic rope with a hot knife or match, and remove the tape.

RING SPLICE

This splice attaches the working end of a rope to a ring or clew. Chafing between the ring and strands is minimal if the first round of tucks is pulled tight. Many sailors and fishermen use it to attach rope to chain, but directions for a safer, more professional Rope-to-Chain splice are given in chapter 11.

TOOLS AND MATERIALS

Three-strand twisted rope
Swedish fid
Ring
Vinyl tape or whipping twine
Scissors or sharp knife
Hot knife or heat source
Ruler

Unlay the rope 2 or 3 inches (50 to 80 mm) and tape or seize each of the individual strands. Tape where the unlaying is to end. For ³/₄-inch (19 mm) rope, that would be 12 inches (0.3 m) from the working end for a three-tuck splice; 16 inches (0.4 m) for four tucks. Unlay the rope to the tape.

Pass the first strand on the left (Strand A) through the ring from front to back and around the ring, coming out to the right of itself. Work Strands B and C the same way, then pass Strand C to the left, over itself, and back between itself and Strand B. Draw up this round of tucks tightly and remove the tape.

To work the second round of tucks, pick up the middle strand

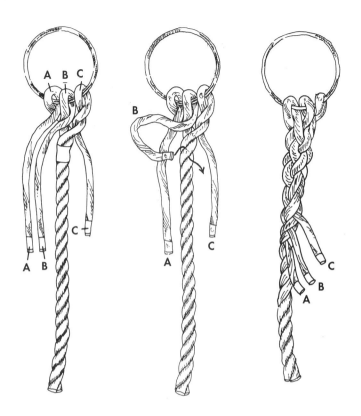

(B), pass it over the base of the third strand (C), and tuck it under the strand below (A).

Pick up the working end of Strand A, then pass it over Strand B and under the strand below. It will come out where Strand B tucked in on this second round. Remove the tape.

For a smooth, better-looking splice, finish with the California method: After three or four full rounds of tucks (five with nylon rope), the first strand is left as is. The next strand is tucked once and the last strand is tucked twice.

Cut the ends off close, seal or melt the ends of synthetic rope with a hot knife or match.

SHORT SPLICE

This is the strongest splice for putting two lengths of twisted rope together. The rope thickens at the splice, so it should not be used when a line must pass over an exact-sized pulley or through an opening only slightly larger than itself. In these situations, it is better to use a whole length of rope.

TOOLS AND MATERIALS

Three-strand twisted rope (two pieces)
Swedish fid
Vinyl tape or whipping twine
Scissors or sharp knife
Hot knife or heat source
Ruler

Unlay one end of each rope for 2 or 3 inches (50 to 80 mm) and tape or seize the six individual ends. Continue unlaying; for ³/₄-inch (19 mm) rope, 16 inches (0.4 m) in each rope is ample for a four-tuck splice. Tape to prevent the ropes from unlaying farther.

Interlace, or marry, the two pieces of rope so that each strand is parallel to the corresponding strand of the other piece. To hold the splice together, place a temporary seizing of tape or twine where the two pieces join.

The first tuck of the round is started by placing one strand over the standing part of its corresponding strand and under the next. In most cases, this can be done with your fingers, but if the rope is twisted too tightly, use the Swedish fid to smooth the way.

Rotate the work and repeat until all three strands are tucked. One round of tucks is now complete; finish the other side of the seizing in the same way.

Remove the seizing and tighten the splice by pulling on the strand ends.

Repeat all the tucks three more times. For nylon rope, continue for a total of five or six rounds.

For a smooth, better-looking splice, finish with the California method: After four full rounds of tucks, the first strand is left as is. The next strand is tucked once and the last strand is tucked twice.

Cut the ends off close, seal or melt the ends of synthetic rope with a hot knife or match, and remove the tape.

Three-Strand Short Splice

END SPLICE

The bitter end of a rope is often finished with whipping; this splice is a good alternative when improved grip is important.

TOOLS AND MATERIALS

Three-strand twisted rope
Swedish fid
Vinyl tape or whipping twine
Scissors or sharp knife
Hot knife or heat source
Ruler

Unlay about 3 inches (75 mm) of rope and tape or seize the individual ends. Tape where the unlaying should end. For this splice in ³/₄-inch (19 mm) rope, that would be about 16 inches (0.4 m) from the working end for a four-tuck splice. Unlay the rope to the tape.

Hold the rope at the tape between your thumb and forefinger with the strands emerging upward and spreading over the top of your fist, like the petals of a flower.

To begin, crown the three strands. To do this, take any strand and, moving counterclockwise, lead it over the strand next to it (we will call this the *second strand*). Allow the resultant bight, or loop, to remain prominent, because you will need it later.

The second strand leads over the first strand, then over the third strand. This third strand then leads over the second strand and down through the bight formed in your first step. The crown is now complete; draw it up tightly.

Remove the tape or seizing. For the first round of tucks, raise a strand on the standing part of the line and insert any adjacent working strand under it. You can usually do this with your fingers, but if the rope is twisted too tightly, use a Swedish fid.

Tuck a working end over the strand you just tucked under, and under the strand just below it.

Turn the entire piece over. You have one working strand left to tuck, and there is one strand left in the standing part of the rope that doesn't have a working strand under it. Make this tuck, continuing to work counter to the lay of the rope.

The first round of tucks is now complete. Tighten if necessary by pulling on the strand ends.

Repeat the series of tucks three more times, unless the rope is nylon, which holds better with five or six rounds.

For a smooth, better-looking splice, finish with the California method: After the rounds of tucks are complete, the first strand is left as is. The next strand is tucked once (as in the beginning steps) and the last strand is tucked twice.

Cut the ends off close, seal or melt the ends of synthetic rope with a hot knife or match, and remove the tape.

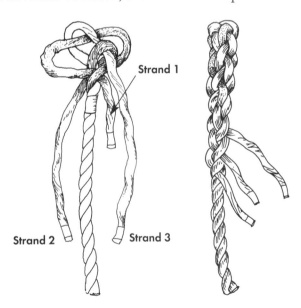

THREE-STRAND SPLICING PROJECTS

These splicing projects are fun as well as practical, but shop carefully for your rope so you don't work for hours and then end up with a frazzled mess. If necessary, spend a few cents more for good-quality, three-strand twisted rope or small stuff.

Use ¼-inch (6 mm) nylon or spun Dacron for the key lanyard and leash and collar; use manila or combination rope for the railing. Ask the salesperson to unlay a short portion of the rope after heat-sealing or taping the three strands and check to see that each strand holds its individual twist. If the yarns fly apart, or if the rope does not retain its shape, search for better rope. Remember to ask the salesperson to tape the rope to keep it from unlaying farther on your trip home.

KEY LANYARD

This is a simple, attractive lanyard to hold keys or a knife.

TOOLS AND MATERIALS

Three-strand small stuff: 26 inches (650 mm) of
³⁄₁₆- or ¼-inch (5 to 6 mm) rope
Ring
Vinyl tape or whipping twine
Scissors or sharp knife
Ruler

A 26-inch (650 mm) piece of small stuff will give you a finished lanyard length of about 12 inches (300 mm). Attach the ring using the ring splice with at least five tucks; allow 6 inches (150 mm) for the splice. On the other end, form the loop, allowing 8 inches (200 mm) for the decorative eye splice with five tucks.

Directions for the ring splice and decorative eye splice are given in chapter 2.

DOG COLLAR AND LEASH

This is a classy but inexpensive set for your dog.

TOOLS AND MATERIALS

Three-strand twisted rope
1 or 2 Rings
Spring-tension clip
Vinyl tape or whipping twine
Scissors or sharp knife
Ruler

For a collar of ½-inch (12 mm) rope, allow enough to comfortably encircle the dog's neck, plus 12 inches (300 mm) for the splices.

For a loose collar, attach both ends of the collar to the same ring using ring splices. For a choke-style collar, use a ring splice to attach a ring to each end of the collar.

Allow 5½ feet (1.7 m) of rope for a 4-foot (1.2 m) leash. Attach the clip to one end using a ring splice. Finish the other end with an eye splice, making the eye large enough for your hand.

Directions for the ring splice and eye splice are given in chapter 2.

ROPE RAILINGS WITH DOUBLE WALL AND CROWN KNOT

This is an unusually pretty way to frame a favorite area in the garden or to line a walkway. It can also be used as an inexpensive safety railing around docks and piers. The double wall and crown knot serves as a stop-knot where the rope passes through a post.

TOOLS AND MATERIALS

Three-strand twisted rope
Vinyl tape or whipping twine
Scissors or sharp knife
Ruler

For directions on tying the double wall and crown knot, see the decorative eye splice in chapter 2.

CLIFF'S SAILING HARNESS

My friend Cliff gave me the pattern for this smart harness, which is easy and inexpensive to make. The harness is light and takes up very little room when not in use. Dacron works best for this; nylon tends to shrink and harden with age and wetting.

TOOLS AND MATERIALS

25 Feet (7.6 m) of ⅜-inch (9 mm) three-strand Dacron rope
1 Heavy-duty snaphook
Tape
Sharp knife or scissors
Whipping twine and needle

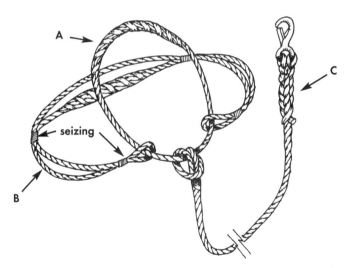

The harness consists of three pieces: an endless loop that fits over the shoulders (A), another endless loop that, when doubled, goes around your trunk (B), and a tether with snaphook (C).

To make A, cut off a length of rope 40 inches (1.02 m) long. On both ends, measure back from the end 4 inches (100 mm) and tape at that spot. Unlay both ends back to the tape, taking care to preserve the three strands. Execute a short splice, as described in chapter 2. Three rounds of tucks on each side are adequate for this purpose.

To make B, you will need to get your chest measurements, over foul-weather gear if need be. Double the measurements; to that amount, add 10 inches (250 mm). Cut the second piece of rope equal to that measurement. Execute another short splice in this piece, but only after wrapping each end around endless loop A. Secure piece B with four seizings, as visible in the drawing on the previous page.

The rope that remains is for the tether, which should be long enough to let you move around but short enough to keep you in or within reach of the boat. Ten feet or thereabouts is a common compromise. At one end, splice in a 4-inch (100 mm) eye; at the other end, splice in a 9-inch (225 mm) eye. The splices on this piece should have five rounds of tucks.

FOUR

DOUBLE-BRAID ROPE

Double-braid is the most common and widely used configuration of ropes made from polyester, aramid (Kevlar), and polyethylene (Spectra). Double-braid rope is composed of a braided core inside a braided coat, or outer covering. Sometimes various materials are blended to optimize such qualities as strength, weight, stretch, and cost. For example, rope with a Spectra-aramid core and polyester coat is as strong as 7 × 19 wire of half the diameter, stretches about the same, and weighs less. But no matter the materials used, both core and coat contribute to the strength of the rope. It is important, therefore, that when your splice is finished, the coat covers the core smoothly and evenly, as it did when manufactured. To accomplish this, be sure to tie a Slip Knot, as directed for each splice, to keep the core from sliding up inside the cover while you work.

The weak spot on spliced rope lies on the standing side of the splice, where the rope is first disturbed. Tapered ends are usually buried there, so follow the tapering directions carefully.

EYE SPLICE

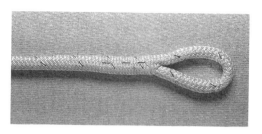

Follow these steps to put an eye or thimble at the end of double-braid rope.

TOOLS AND MATERIALS

Double-braid rope
Tubular fid
Vinyl tape
Scissors or sharp knife
Marking pen
Waxed whipping twine
Needle
Thimble (optional)

Trim the end of the rope evenly, cutting off melted ends, or tape the end to be spliced. Using a tubular fid (see page 12), measure one full fid length from the tape and label this point with an R. (To determine the appropriate fid for the rope you are using, see page 12.)

Add the amount of rope necessary to form the eye or the loop around the thimble (see page 16), if one is used. Mark an X there, at the throat of the splice. This is a complicated splice to complete with a thimble, so measurements are critical.

Move up the rope at least five full fid lengths and tie a tight slip knot.

Return to the X and gently push aside the strands of the coat (the rope's outer covering) to expose its inner core. Pull a small loop of the core through the coat as carefully as possible, and draw a single hash mark across the core. Then continue pulling out the core until its working end is completely exposed, and tape the end. Work the cover down into place to confirm that the X and hash mark are aligned and equal distances from the coat and core end, respectively.

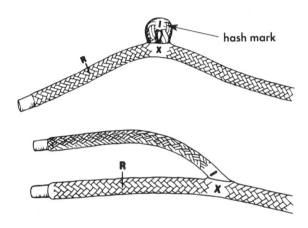

Now pull out more core, this time from the standing part of the rope, and measure one short fid length from the single hash mark. (Short and long fid lengths are marked on tubular fids; for the measurement in inches, see page 12.) Make two hash marks there (see drawing next page).

Continue along the core for one full fid length plus one short fid length, pulling out more from the standing part if necessary. Make three hash marks.

For maximum strength in the splice, you will need to draw the rope's outer coat into its core and then its core into the coat. It will help to remember that the coat is marked with letters and the core with hash marks.

Pinch the taped end of the coat and insert it into the hollow end of the fid, taping it in place. Push the fid into the core at two hash marks and out at three hash marks. Be careful not to twist the coat. Pull until the R comes into view. The core will bunch up as you do so, but this will correct itself later.

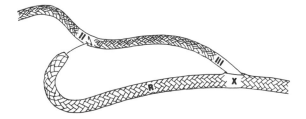

To taper the end of the coat, work toward the fid from R, and count off seven sets of picks, or parallel ribs, that run clockwise; mark this spot with a T. Continue toward the fid, marking every seventh pair with a dot so you will know where to cut.

Now go back to the R, this time marking the counterclockwise picks for tapering. To offset the tapering on these picks, mark your first dot at the fourth pair. From there, mark every seventh counterclockwise pair until you reach the fid.

Remove the fid and the tape. Cut and remove a single strand at each marked pick along the coat.

While holding the core, pull the coat until the T shows beyond the two hash marks. Take care not to lose the end of the tapered coat into the core.

For extra strength, the core end should be drawn through the coat, past the throat of the splice, and into the standing part of the rope. Measure from the X toward the slip knot one short half of the tubular fid; label this spot with a Z.

Tape the pinched end of the core into the hollow fid end. Insert it into the coat at the T and work it through the coat as far as you can without a struggle. Depending on the size of the eye, the fid may not reach the necessary exit point in one pass. If this happens, bring the fid out of the coat, pulling some of the core with it. Then simply reinsert the fid into the *same* hole and work it farther through the coat. Continue this snaking process until the fid exits at the Z. Be sure not to snag any strands of coat with the fid at reentry points.

Draw up the slack until the coat-to-core unions formed at the T and two hash marks meet at the top of the eye. Now that this portion of the splice is complete, you should hide the end of the coat by smoothing the coat from the T to the three hash marks. Take your time and be thorough so the tapered end slides completely into the core at the three hash marks.

Remove the fid and smooth the pucker. Poke through the coat at the X to make some visible mark on the core inside. Also mark the core where it exits from the Z. Pull on the core tail until the mark you made under the X exits from the coat at the Z. Unbraid the tail, comb and fan it; then cut it off at a 45-degree angle between the two marks. Hold the rope gently at the union, and ease the coat from there around the eye until the core tail disappears. Trim the ends.

Take a firm grip of the rope close to the slip knot or attach it with a hook to a firm surface. If you measured carefully from the beginning of the splice, there should be enough slack in the bunched coat to roll down of the tail end and the coat-to-core joints.

Bunching may occur at the throat as the doubled core section and displaced yarns are distributed. If it does, roll and flex the rope or gently tug on the tail of the core. Begin this process gently but firmly. As you proceed, you may have to exert more pressure, perhaps to the point of pounding on the throat with a wooden mallet.

Double-braid splices—like most splices—are easy to take apart because they are designed to be pulled on, not pushed. To hold this splice firm, lock-stitch it in the following way.

Pass a needle threaded with twine all the way through the throat, leaving a tail of about 8 inches (200 mm). Make three complete stitches running along the standing part of the rope. Remove the needle from the twine and thread it with the tail end. Sew three stitches parallel to the first, but 90 degrees around the rope's circumference from them. Bring the two ends together through the standing part of the rope and tie with a square knot, shown in chapter 15.

Turn the rope 90 degrees and repeat the stitches. Trim the twine ends.

If you wish to protect the eye with a leather chafing strip, you'll need to apply this before you put in the lock-stitching (see chapter 13).

In the 1960s, Samson Ropes, now the American Group (Ferndale WA), developed a superior rope double braid. The quality of the product is excellent, and the price is reasonable.

END-TO-END SPLICE

Here is a way to make an endless loop or to join pieces of double-braid rope.

TOOLS AND MATERIALS

Double-braid rope
Tubular fid
Vinyl tape
Scissors or sharp knife
Marking pen
Needle

To make an endless loop in double-braid rope, you should allow four full fid lengths of rope to accommodate the splice. (See page 12 for the relationship between rope diameter and fid size.) Do not use double-braid for an endless loop smaller than 2½ feet (750 mm) in circumference; for those splices, use three-strand twisted, eight-plait, or twelve-plait rope.

For maximum strength of an end-to-end splice, it is essential that the smooth, one-to-one relationship between coat and core be restored as completely as possible. This can be difficult, but pounding on the rope with a wooden mallet will loosen the strands and ease the job.

On each piece, draw the coat down over the working end of the core, removing as much slack as possible from the coat. Cut each end so that the coat and core are the same length, and tape to prevent unlaying.

Measure six full tubular fid lengths from each end and tie a slip knot.

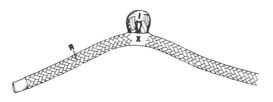

Measure one full fid length from each end and label these reference points with an R. (Short and long fid lengths are marked on tubular fids; for the measurements in inches, see page 12.)

Mark an X one short fid length up the standing part of each rope from the R.

At the X, gently push aside the strands of the coat to expose its inner core. Pull out a small loop of core through the coat as carefully as possible, and draw a single hash mark across the top of the core.

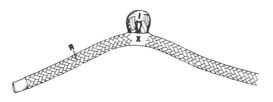

Pull out the working-end core completely at the X and tape its end. Smooth the coat and core to confirm that the X and hash mark are aligned at equal distances from the end. Now pull out more core—this time from the standing part of the rope—and measure one short fid length from the single hash mark. Draw two hash marks there (see page 47).

Continue along the core, pulling out more from the standing part if necessary, and mark three hash marks at a distance totaling one full fid length plus one short fid length from the two-hash-mark point.

Repeat with the second rope.

To taper the coats, work with each separately. From the R, toward the working end, count off seven sets of picks, or parallel ribs, that run clockwise and mark this spot with a T. Continue to work toward the end, placing a dot at *every other* clockwise pick until five have been marked, so you will know where to cut.

Beginning again at the T, mark every other counterclockwise pick.

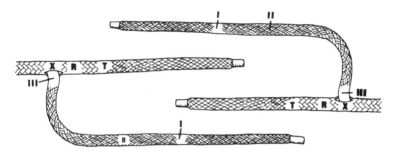

Cut and remove the marked strands between the T and the working end. Untape the end while pulling the strand loose. Repeat with the second rope.

Pinch the taped end of either coat and insert it into the hollow end of the fid; tape it in place. Push the fid into the core of the *other* rope at two hash marks and out at three hash marks, being careful not to twist the coat. While holding the core, pull until the T is aligned with the two hash marks. Some bunching of the core will occur, but this will resolve itself later.

Repeat this procedure with the second rope.

Each core must now be reinserted into the coat that runs through its center. Tape the pinched end of either core into the hollow fid end and insert the fid at the T. Work it through the coat and exit at the X. Repeat with the other rope.

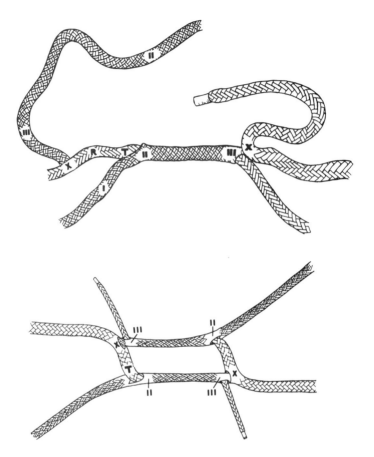

Draw up the slack by pulling on both core and coat tails until the coat-to-core crossovers are snug.

Hold the rope at a joint and smooth all the puckered braid, working in both directions away from the joint. Take your time and be thorough so the tapered end of the coat slides completely into the core at three hash marks. Remove the fid from the core tail. Repeat with the second joint.

Cut off the core tails flush at the coat.

Take a firm grip of the rope close to a slip knot. If you measured carefully from the beginning of the splice, there should be enough slack in the coat to pull down over one of the coat-to-core joints and the tail ends. Repeat to cover the second joint with slack from the opposite direction.

Bunching may occur as all the extra yarns running through the coat are distributed. If it does, roll and flex the rope. Begin this process gently but firmly, gradually applying more pressure as necessary. You may have to pound the rope with a wooden mallet.

An opening through the splice is normal, but it should not be any longer than the diameter of the rope.

Lock-stitch with needle and thread (see page 44).

END SPLICE

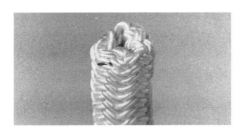

This is a neat alternative to whipping a double-braid rope.

TOOLS AND MATERIALS

Double-braid rope
Tubular fid
Vinyl tape or whipping twine
Scissors or sharp knife
Marking pen

If the end of the rope has been heat-sealed, cut it off and tape it to keep it from unlaying. Measure one full fid length from the working end of the rope and mark this spot with an X.

Move up the rope at least five full fid lengths and tie a tight slip knot.

Return to the X and gently push aside the strands of the coat to expose its inner core. Pull out a small loop of core through the coat as carefully as possible, and make a single hash mark across the top of the core. Pull out the core completely and tape its end. Confirm that the X and hash mark are aligned at equal distances from the end.

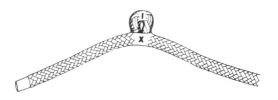

Now pull out more core, this time from the standing part of the rope, and measure one short fid length from the single hash mark. (Short and long fid lengths are marked on tubular fids; for the measurement in inches, see page 12.) Make two hash marks there.

Continue along the core, pulling out more from the standing part of the rope if necessary, and make three hash marks at a distance totaling one full fid length plus one short fid length from the two hash marks.

Now draw the rope's outer coat into its core. Remember that the coat is marked with letters, the core with hash marks. Pinch the taped end of the coat and insert it into the hollow end of the fid; tape it in place. Push the fid into the core at two hash marks and out at three. Be careful not to twist the coat. Pull until the splice is snug but not buckled.

Remove the fid and tape. To taper the coat tail, unbraid and fan it, then mark one-third of a full fid length up the coat. Cut at an angle from the opposite bottom corner.

Smooth the core, working from two to three hash marks; if you measured carefully, the coat tail will slip into the core.

Starting from the slip knot, work the coat down over the core, pulling an ever-deepening fold into the coat ahead of your fingers. When you reach the end, the fold you have created should be deep enough to envelope the entire splice. The crease of the fold where it terminates at the working end of the splice will appear like the half-inverted finger of a rubber glove when you slip it off your hand.

Cut the core off flush with the coat. Smooth it again to ensure that any exposed core is completely covered.

ROPE-TO-WIRE SPLICE

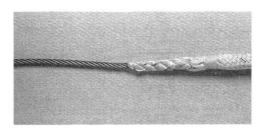

A Rope-to-Wire Splice is often used to attach rigging wire to a halyard. With double-braid rope, both the core and coat must be spliced into the wire.

TOOLS AND MATERIALS

Double-braid rope
7 × 19 Stainless steel wire
Swedish fid
Wire cutters
Vinyl tape
Scissors or sharp knife
Hot knife or flame source
Ruler
Waxed whipping twine
Marking pen
Homemade splicing jig (optional)

The 7 × 19 stainless steel wire consists of six strands, each containing 19 yarns, and a central core. The wire should be suitable for rigging and should measure about one-half the rope's diameter.

For this splice, the wire must be tapered to a core plus one strand.

Cut one strand at 6 inches (150 mm) from the end, one at 5 inches (125 mm), one at 4 inches (100 mm), and two at 3 inches (75 mm). Tape around the wire at each level.

Tie a slip knot 8 feet (2.4 m) up the braided rope to keep the coat from creeping up the core more than necessary. If the end of the rope has been heat-sealed, cut it off; push the coat 4 feet (1.2 m) up the core. Cut off 6 inches (150 mm) of the exposed core and tape the end.

Measure up the core 21 inches (530 mm) and mark.

Insert the tip of the tapered wire into the hollow core 8 inches (200 mm) from the working end, and gently and carefully work it up through the core until it reaches the mark at 21 inches (530 mm).

Tape lightly around the core and wire at the 21- and 8-inch (530 and 200 mm) locations to hold your work snug. (From this point on, the work will go more smoothly with a jig, which I'll describe in the next section.)

Working carefully, unbraid the core to the 8-inch (200 mm) mark and divide the yarns into three groups. You will get a much neater splice if you tape neighboring yarns together.

To splice the first group of yarns into the wire, slip the fid under two wire strands in the direction *opposite* the twist of the wire (see drawing page 54). Lay the rope along the groove from the handle to the tip; pull the rope into place and remove the tool. Repeat with the other two yarn groups, carrying on around the back of the wire to make a complete wrap with each group. Continue until three rounds of tucks are completed. Remove one-third of each group and tuck the fourth round; remove another third and tuck the fifth round. Cut the ends very close.

Melt any ends into the wire by passing a lighted match *close* to the cut ends. Use some care here or you could melt your whole splice.

Beginning at the slip knot, milk the coat by squeezing it while sliding your hand gradually toward the wire. Work in short, overlapping sections and do not pull on the coat. When you have removed all slack, the core-to-wire portion of the splice should be completely covered. Whip over the coat where the splice on the core ends. (Instructions for whipping are given in chapter 13.)

For the coat-to-wire portion of the splice, unbraid the coat, smooth the yarns out straight, and—as you did previously with the core—divide the yarns into three groups. These groups must also be spliced into the wire, but they will be inserted so they travel in the same direction as the wire strands. Insert each group under the appropriate wire-strand pair, completing one round of tucks.

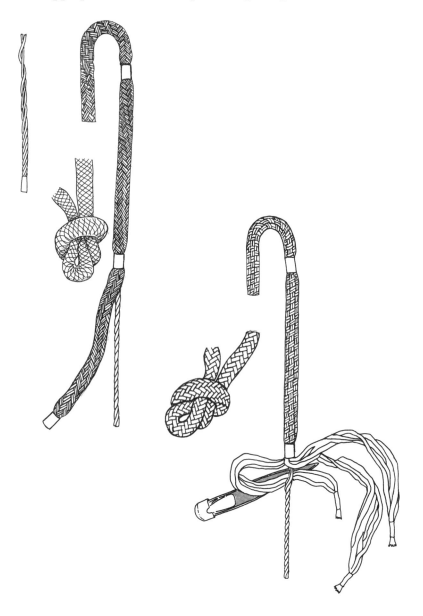

To taper this splice, repeat the tucks, omitting a portion of each yarn group at each tuck, until only a few yarns remain. Cut the ends close to the wire and carefully melt the yarn ends with a match.

JIG FOR THE
ROPE-TO-WIRE SPLICE

A jig supplies me with an extra pair of hands that never gets tired when I'm doing rope-to-wire splicing. To make it, you'll need the following materials:

TOOLS AND MATERIALS

1 Length of 1 × 5½ x 24-inch wood (25 × 140 × 610 mm)

2 Pieces of common 2 × 8s
(actual dimensions 1⅝ × 7½ inches/41 × 190 mm),
5½ inches (140 mm) long

2 Hinges
2 Perko #769 Clamp Stays (available at any good marine store)
6 Wood screws, #8 × 2½ inches (64 mm)
Screws for hinges and clamp stays
2 Bolts (cap screws) ⁵⁄₁₆ x 2½ inches (8 × 64 mm)
1 Pair of 6-inch (150 mm) pointed-nose vise grips
1 Pair of 6-inch (150 mm) regular vise grips
2 Pieces of ½-inch (12 mm) copper tubing, ¾ inch (19 mm) long

Start by drilling a ½-inch (12 mm) hole through each 2 × 8, centered at midlength (2¾ inches/70 mm from either end) and approximately 1½ inches (38 mm) down from the top edge. Along the lower semicircular arc, 2 inches (50 mm) from the center of each ½-inch hole, drill about five ⁵⁄₁₆-inch (8 mm) holes.

Next, saw off the tops of the two 2 × 8s and save. The cuts should be 1½ inches (38 mm) down from the top edges, through the centers of the ½-inch (12 mm) holes.

Install the saved tops, using the hinges and the clamp stays.

Now screw the two 2 × 8s upright to the 24-inch (610 mm) piece of wood using the #8 × 2½-inch (64 mm) screws. On my jig, I installed one of the 2 × 8s 1 inch (25 mm) from one end, and the other 6 inches (150 mm) from the other end, but these dimensions are a matter of preference. Leaving some space at the ends will allow you to clamp the jig to a work surface.

Once the jig is together, you will realize that you no longer have two true ½-inch (12 mm) holes where the wire and rope go through, because the board was cut directly at the holes. It will be beneficial if you run your ½-inch drill through them again while they are clamped shut.

To keep splinters at bay and to help your rope from becoming snagged, sand the entire jig and round the edges and corners slightly.

Pound the two pieces of copper tubing over the jaws of the 6-inch (150 mm) regular vise grips, one piece on each jaw. This will help prevent damage to the wire.

Wrap the jaws of the pointed-nose vise grips with electrician's tape to help prevent damage to the rope.

Set your piece into the jig, positioning the rope-to-wire marriage at the center. Clamp the copper-clad vise grips onto the wire on the outside of the upright, flat against the wood. If your wire is of small diameter, you might notice that it floats around in the hole. I cure this by taping in a "bushing" of leather or cardboard. Next, clamp the pointed-nose grips onto the rope; again, outside the upright and flat against the wood. Insert a bolt into one of the ⁵⁄₁₆-inch (8 mm) holes so the vise grips cannot spin around. You'll know on what side to set it in just a moment.

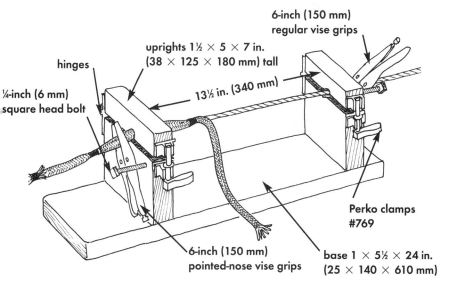

6-inch (150 mm) regular vise grips

uprights 1½ × 5 × 7 in. (38 × 125 × 180 mm) tall

hinges

¼-inch (6 mm) square head bolt

13½ in. (340 mm)

Perko clamps #769

6-inch (150 mm) pointed-nose vise grips

base 1 × 5½ × 24 in. (25 × 140 × 610 mm)

Our next job is to ease some twist out of the wire. Rotate the copper-clad vise grips so that the lay of the wire loosens. Note: if the pointed vise grips on the rope rotate along with the copper-clad vise grips, the wire won't unlay, so set the bolt as described. The wire will start dipping and curving; some wires do this more than others. I have found that some wires need two full rotations while others need only a half turn. When you think you have a little of the twist removed, stop the copper-clad grips with a bolt. Take care here because if the grips slip out of your hand, it will whirl around, knocking your knuckles with some force. You will be able to tuck only once or twice before having to adjust the grips again.

CORE-TO-CORE EYE SPLICE

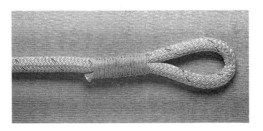

Use this alternative eye splice on double-braid rope such as Kevlar or Spectra for which—according to the manufacturers' specifications—the primary strength lies in the core.

TOOLS AND MATERIALS

Double-braid rope
Tubular fid
Vinyl tape
Scissors or sharp knife
Marking pen
Waxed whipping twine
Needle
Thimble (optional)

Place a fresh piece of tape on the rope end where the eye is to be spliced to keep the rope from unlaying. Using a tubular fid, measure two full fid lengths from the tape and label this reference point with an R.

Add the amount of rope necessary to form the eye, or for the loop around the thimble, if one is used. Mark an X here, at the throat of the splice. (This is a complicated splice to complete with a thimble, so measurements are critical.)

Move up the rope at least eight full fid lengths and tie a tight slip knot.

Return to the X and gently push aside the strands of the coat to expose its inner core. Pull out a small loop of core through the coat as carefully as possible. Draw a single hash mark across the top of the core.

Pull out the working-end core completely, and tape its end.

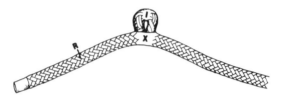

Now pull out more core, this time from the standing part of the rope, and measure one short fid length from the single hash mark. Make two hash marks there.

Continue along the core three full fid lengths plus one short fid length, pulling out more core if necessary. Make three hash marks.

Pinch the taped end of the core and insert it into the hollow end of the fid; tape it in place. Push the fid into the coat at the R and out at the X. You should now have the core exiting twice at the X. Pull the core through until the single hash mark lines up with the R, then hold it firmly in position while you smooth the coat from the R to the X. Mark the tail core where it exits at the X with a band around the core.

Insert the fid (with the core end still taped to it) into the core at the two hash marks, run it through the core, and pull it out at the three hash marks—in effect, pulling the core through itself. Pull until the band lines up with the two hash marks.

To taper the tail that exits at the three hash marks, fan it. Then measure from its working end one-third of a full fid length, making a mark at that point. Cut at an angle from the opposite bottom corner to the place marked.

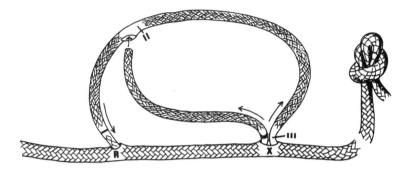

**The distance between I and II is one short fid length.
The distance between II and III is three full
fid lengths plus one short fid length.**

Hold the rope where the band on the core and the two hash marks meet, and smooth the core toward the loose tail. The tail should slip into the core if your measurements were correct.

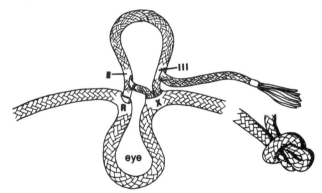

Core disappears into coat at X.

Attach the slip knot to a sturdy hook, or have an assistant hold it. Smooth the coat from the knot toward the splice until the whole core is enveloped by the coat, taking special care around the eye. Detach the slip knot from the hook, and attach the eye there instead.

Pull tightly both the standing part of the rope and the coat tail (from the R to the working end) toward you.

Apply a tight layer of tape around the throat for a distance equal to one short fid length.

Apply a tight whipping over the tape (see chapter 13).

Cut the tail close.

REDUCED VOLUME
END-TO-END SPLICE

Kim Houghton, owner of Rig-Rite, introduced me to this splice recently. Some sailboat roller-furler mechanisms require an endless loop of line for operation, and sometimes the endless-loop splice built using the manufacturer's recommended method is too bulky to reeve through the furler drum. The splice shown here has a 50 percent smaller cross section than the standard splice. Its strength is also reduced by 50 percent, but it remains strong enough for the purpose.

TOOLS AND MATERIALS

Double-braid rope
Tubular fid to suit your rope
Tape
Marking pen
Sharp knife or scissors
Whipping twine and needle

Before executing this splice, reeve the line around the drum and through all the relevant hardware. Assuming you're leading the line back to the cockpit, you'll need the length of the endless loop to be twice the distance from drum to cockpit, plus the extra needed for the drum, the cockpit belay, and any intervening directional changes.

If the rope ends have been heat-sealed, cut off the sealed ends, then tape them to keep them from unlaying. Lay the ends out and mark the rope at two places toward each end: Mark A should be one full fid length from the ends; Mark B should be half a full fid length from Mark A.

Put a good, tight, permanent whipping right behind each of the two B marks. Now, just in front of the two B marks, separate the coat strands to expose the core. Pry them out completely and cut off the core tails flush at the coat.

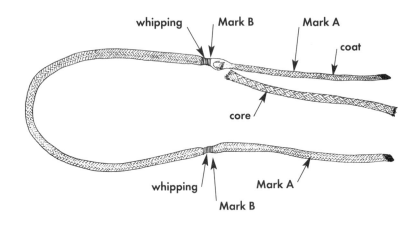

Using the fid, marry the two taped ends by interlacing one into the other at the mid-point A marks. The taped ends exit the coat at the B marks. Thoroughly milk out all the slack.

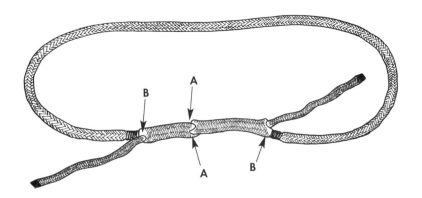

Cut the ends close, and sew the crossover at Mark B.

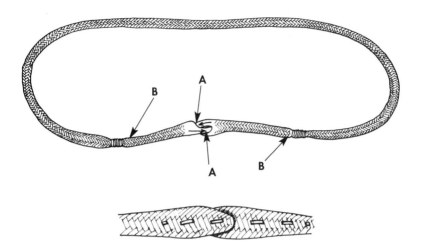

FIVE

SOLID-BRAID SPLICE

This interesting splice proves that it's possible to put an eye at the end of any rope, no matter the construction.

Until World War II, rope always consisted of combed plant fibers that were twisted by stages into three strands, which in turn were twisted into a single length of rope. But then rope manufacturers found that braiding rather than twisting the strands created a smoother rope that was less prone to chafe and wear. The first such ropes were window-sash cords, from which came all sorts of single-braid cordage (also known as solid-braid because it is of uniform cross-sectional construction, without a core or hollow center). Single-braid was soon supplanted for most purposes by today's incomparable double-braid ropes, in which an equally tensioned cover and core offer great strength and ease of splicing. We still see nylon or polyester single-braid in use for clotheslines and other light-duty tasks, however.

I learned the solid-braid splice by way of a bet. Shortly after the first edition of this book was published, Ron Denise from South Carolina visited my shop. His specialty is providing ropes, slings, and harnesses for arborists. He stayed a week, opening my eyes to a whole different world of rigging. One day, with a wicked gleam in his eye, he said, "I can splice any rope you give me." I dug around and found a length of hard-used ¼-inch (6 mm) clothesline and handed it to him, saying, "We all know it's impossible to splice hard-used rope, and this small-diameter single-braid should make it even more interesting. Good luck!" Then I watched while he set in a solid-braid splice. Ron called it a *helical splice*—I suppose because the weave twists around and down the rope barber-pole fashion.

I've since seen these splices used to set in the eyes of the puller ropes used by utility companies, and in lengths of rubber-coated ropes used in some places in fishing nets and gear. On pleasure boats, I've seen this splice set in flag halyards.

If the rope you're splicing is to be used under severe conditions, such as high loads or rough handling, contact the rope manufacturer for its latest splicing instructions and recommendations.

TOOLS AND MATERIALS

Braided rope (flag halyard)
Scissors or sharp knife
Whipping twine and needle
Waterproof flexible adhesive (such as that made by 3M)
Marking pen (fine)

The method of measuring is different from other splices. Instead of fid lengths, we will be using rope diameters.

Lay out your rope, forming an eye of the desired size and leaving a tail of the necessary length. To determine the length of strands necessary for the splice, measure the diameter of the rope. Allow a length of 22 rope diameters for the tail and make a mark. Remove the tape or cut off the melted end of the rope. Unlay the rope up to the mark. Don't be surprised if the unlaid portion seems unusually long: for this splice it is necessary. Again form the eye and apply a very tight seizing at the throat, measuring three rope diameters. In the illustration, the top half of the seizing is a French Hitching. To make the French hitching, which stays in place nicely especially when working with small cordage, simply tuck the end under each turn of the seizing to make a series of half hitches, with each hitch seated upon the previous one. When you snug the hitches, they should describe a smooth spiral around the rope.

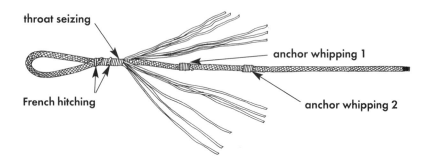

On the standing part of the rope, put a whipping six rope diameters down from the throat and a second whipping six rope diameters down from the beginning of the first. We'll call these *anchor whippings*, because their function is to provide grip points along the slick standing part.

Pick up the strands at the throat and divide them into four groups.

Apply a light coating of adhesive on the standing part of the rope (where you'll be making the splice), taking care to avoid spraying the strands. Essentially, you'll be "braiding" the silky, slippery strands down around the standing part; the adhesive coating (think of it as hair spray!), while not necessary, will make the job easier. Along with the anchor whippings, it will help keep the splice in place while you tie it.

Choose one of the strand groups and wrap it down the standing part of the rope in barber-pole fashion. Fasten the end temporarily with a Constrictor Knot (see inset illustration) below the second whipping. Choose another group and wrap it down the rope in the opposite direction from the first group. Fasten that group with a constrictor knot adjacent to the first constrictor.

Wrap the third and fourth groups of strands in the same fashion, and anchor them temporarily with additional constrictor knots.

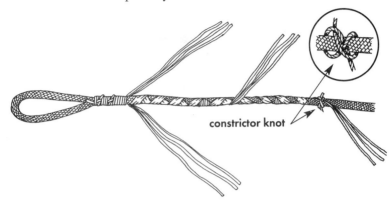

constrictor knot

Over the four groups, place a tight "cover" whipping just as close as possible down from the first anchor whipping on the standing part of the rope. Similarly, butt another cover whipping against the lower edge of the second anchor whipping. Untie the constrictor knots, and reduce the volume of the four strand-group ends by half.

Pick up the reduced strands and wrap them barber-pole fashion as mentioned previously. Fasten the ends a short distance down from the second whipping, first with a temporary constrictor knot and then a whipping. Cut and remove half the remaining strands from each group. Now you have a tapered splice, and you can end it here by trimming all the strand ends close to the last whipping. Alternatively, if you want an even gentler taper, you can halve the volume of the remaining strand groups yet again, and repeat the last step. Then trim the remaining ends close.

If you like, coat the piece with a light coating of clear spray lacquer or acrylic. After all, a four-strand, plaited, Single-Braid Splice is a true example of marlinspike art.

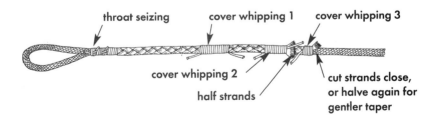

throat seizing   cover whipping 1   cover whipping 3

cover whipping 2

half strands

cut strands close, or halve again for gentler taper

SIX

BRAID WITH THREE-STRAND CORE

Braided rope with three-strand core can also be called 16-plait with three-strand core because the outer coat consists of 16 strands. I like Marlowbraid's fuzzy coat; it provides a good grip and, at the same time, feels good in my hands. Technically a two-part rope, it is unlike double-braid because 90 percent of its strength is in its twisted core.

This is a difficult rope to splice, but the results are worth the extra effort. Don't attempt to splice any rope of this type under $\frac{1}{4}$ inch (6 mm) in diameter, because the Marlow splicing tool (see page 13) won't fit; for smaller rope, use the solid braid splice described in chapter 5.

EYE SPLICE

TOOLS AND MATERIALS

Braid with three-strand core
Marlow splicing tool
Scissors or sharp knife
Vinyl tape
Marking pen
Ruler
Whipping twine
Thimble (optional)
Swedish fid

Tie a slip knot about 5 feet (1.5 m) from the end of the rope to prevent the coat from creeping up the core more than necessary. If the end of the rope has been heat-sealed, cut it off and tape the new end to prevent unlaying.

Mark the coat 9 inches (230 mm) from the end to make room in the working end for the splice. Form the rope into an eye and mark the coat again. (Allow an extra ½ inch/12 mm if you are using a thimble.)

Push aside the threads of the coat at your second mark until the hole is large enough to expose the core. Extract the core by hooking it with a Swedish fid. Cut 3 inches (75 mm) off the core's end.

Form the eye to the proper size, this time on the core, and cut off one of the core's three twisted strands at the throat of the splice.

Move toward the working end an inch (25 mm) or so, and remove *half* the thickness of another strand; tape. Continue tapering and taping until the end of the core is small enough to go through the eye of the splicing tool.

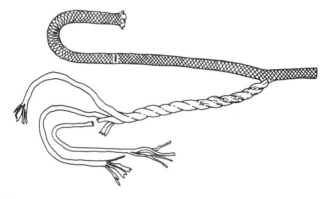

To ease the coat away from the core and make the splice easier to complete, draw out additional core from the standing part of the rope. Extract about 3 inches (75 mm) for ⁵/₁₆- and ³/₈-inch (8 and 9 mm) rope, and 4 inches (100 mm) for ⁷/₁₆- and ¹/₂-inch (11 and 12 mm) rope.

Begin at the slip knot to reposition the coat by milking it firmly while sliding your hand toward the spot where the coat and core separate. This action loosens the core and coat, and makes them easier to work with. Work in short, overlapping sections and do not pull on the coat.

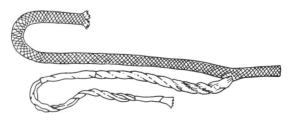

Insert the eye of the Marlow splicing tool (see page 13) into the coat where it opens for the core. Push it through the coat to exit at the throat.

Thread the core through the eye of the splicing tool and draw it back through the coat to exit with the tool at the coat opening.

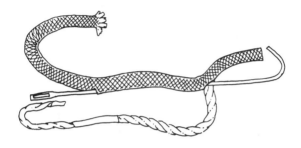

You will now gradually work all of the core ends farther down the standing part of the rope. Untape the ends, unlay the tail, comb out the strands with your fingers, and divide the yarns into three groups. Tape the ends of the new groupings.

Insert the eye of the splicing tool 12 inches (300 mm) below the mark for the throat and exit at the original coat opening. Thread one-third of the tail, located there, into the eye. Pull it through the coat and draw it out.

Repeat with the remaining two sections of core tail, bringing one out 10 inches (250 mm) and the other out 8 inches (200 mm) below the throat, pulling each time. Remove the tape from all three sections.

Pull until the union is firm and the throat closes.

Taper the coat by removing one strand at 3 inches (75 mm) from the end, two strands at 2 inches (50 mm), and four strands at 1 inch (25 mm).

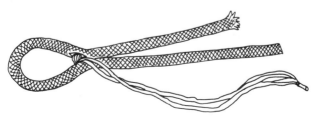

Now the working end of the coat must be pulled through the standing part of the rope. To make it easier to do this, begin a pathway by inserting the empty tool at the throat and pushing it out about 3 inches (75 mm) up the standing part of the rope; wiggle it.

Reverse the tool, entering the rope about 3 inches (75 mm) below the throat and exiting at the throat. Lace the eye with some of the shortest pieces of coat tail and pull them through. Repeat at various points around the circumference, below the throat. Pull the longer tail pieces through farther from the throat.

If you are using a thimble, insert it now. To take the slack out of the splice, hook the eye over a strong hook or knob, hold the core and cover tails, and pull firmly until the coat and core are snug.

Cut off the tails close to their exit points and firmly smooth the entire coat over the core from the slip knot to the throat. The clipped ends should slip into the rope.

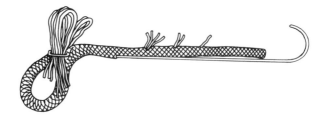

Lock-stitch with needle and thread (see page 44).

ROPE-TO-WIRE SPLICE

This is a good splice to attach rigging wire to a halyard.

TOOLS AND MATERIALS

Braid with three-strand core
7 × 19 Stainless steel wire
Swedish fid
Wire cutters
Vinyl tape
Scissors or sharp knife
Hot knife or flame source
Waxed whipping twine
Marking pen
Ruler
Homemade splicing jig (optional)

The 7 × 19 stainless steel wire consists of six strands, each containing 19 yarns, and a central core. The wire should be suitable for rigging and should measure about one-half the rope's diameter.

For this splice, the wire must be tapered to a core plus one strand. Cut one strand at 6 inches (150 mm) from the end, one at 5 inches (125 mm), one at 4 inches (100 mm), and two at 3 inches (75 mm). Tape around the wire at each level.

Tie a slip knot 8 feet (2.4 m) up the braided rope to keep the coat from creeping up the core more than necessary. If the end of the rope has been heat-sealed, cut it off; push the coat 4 feet (1.2 m) up the core, cut off 6 inches (150 mm) of the exposed core, and tape the end.

Measure 21 inches (530 mm) up the core and tape.

At that point, open the lay and set the tip of tapered wire into the rope's twisted core at a 45-degree angle. Spiral the wire into the lay of the core, continuing to within 6 inches (150 mm) of the working end. Tape into position. Unlay the core strands from here to the working end. (From this point on, the work is easier with a jig to serve as an extra pair of hands. See the jig illustration and instructions under the double-braid rope-to-wire splice in chapter 4 if you'd like to try that route.)

To splice the first rope strand into the wire, slip the fid under two wire strands in the direction *opposite* the twist of the wire. Lay the rope strand along the groove from the handle to the tip; pull the rope into place and remove the tool. For a more finished appearance, untwist the core strand as it passes under the wires.

Repeat with the other two core strands, continuing in a direction opposite the lay of the wires. Each core strand tucks under a different pair of wire strands, just as in a three-strand rope splice. Continue until five rounds of tucks are completed; cut the ends very close.

Beginning at the slip knot, milk the coat by squeezing it while sliding your hand gradually toward the wire. Work in short, overlapping sections, and do not pull on the coat. When you have removed all slack, the core-to-wire portion of the splice should be completely covered. Whip over the coat where the splice on the core ends (instructions for whipping are given in chapter 13).

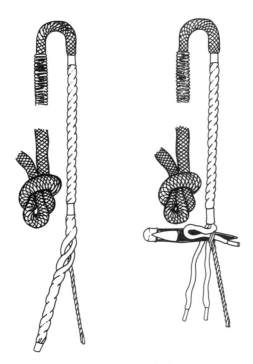

For the coat-to-wire portion of this splice, untwist the coat back to the whipping. Divide the yarns into three groups, trying to keep neighboring yarns together. These yarns must also be spliced into the wire, but they will be inserted so they twist in the *same* direction as the wire.

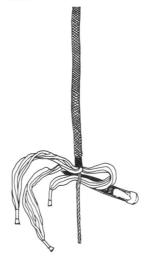

To taper the end, repeat the tucks, omitting one yarn at each tuck until only seven or eight yarns remain in each group.

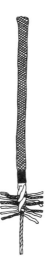

Cut the ends close to the wire.

SEVEN

BRAID WITH PARALLEL CORE

Parallel fibers wrapped in a gauze-like material form the core of this braid. When low stretch and high strength are critical, such as in a halyard, this rope is a good choice; if flexibility is important, double-braid is better.

EYE SPLICE

The basic directions for this splice provide a soft eye that conforms easily to small blocks. A variation, as noted in the following text, produces a hard, unyielding eye that is excellent for situations calling for a larger loop. These directions are for Sta-Set X, manufactured by New England Ropes, Inc., of Fall River, Massachusetts, the major distributor of this rope to the marine market; other braid with parallel core requires a different splice. A special splicing tool, the Uni-Fid (see page 13), is necessary to complete this splice because of the rope's parallel-strand core. Chandleries that stock this rope usually sell the fid also.

TOOLS AND MATERIALS

Braid with parallel core
Uni-Fid
Scissors or sharp knife
Masking tape
Waxed whipping twine
Marking pen

Place a fresh piece of tape on the rope end where the eye is to be spliced to keep the rope from unlaying.

Tie a slip knot 12 full fid lengths from the working end to retain the one-to-one relationship between the core and coat.

Wrap a layer of tape around the rope one full fid length from the working end. (Fid sections are marked on the shipping tube for the tool.) Label this reference point with an R.

Add the amount of rope necessary to form the eye, and mark this spot with an X.

Continuing toward the slip knot, measure 1½ full fid lengths. (Note that one-half of a full fid length is *not* the same as a short fid length.) Mark this point with a Y.

Return to the X and gently pull aside the strands of the coat to expose its inner core. Pull out a small loop using the Uni-Fid. Draw a single hash mark across the top of the core.

Pull out the working-end core completely, taper the end by cutting it at an angle, and tape. This will ease snaking of the core through the coat in a succeeding step.

Now pull out more core, this time from the standing part of the rope, and measure one short fid length from the hash mark. Place two hash marks there.

For a *soft* eye: Place a layer of tape on the standing side of this spot so it just touches the double hash mark.

For a *hard* eye: Measure from the two hash marks toward the working end of the core, the distance between the R and the X (rope set aside for the eye). Place a layer of tape on the standing side of this spot.

Sink the hook of the Uni-Fid into the wrapped core 1½ inches (38 mm) from the tapered end. To prevent snagging, apply a smooth layer of tape to hold the fid in place on the core.

Insert the free end of the fid into the coat at the R and work it past the X, then out through the coat at the Y. Use two hands, massaging the rope ahead of the fid. If you snag the core, back up to free it, and then proceed.

Remove the fid.

Unwind the gauze wrapping from around the parallel fibers of the tail between the tape placed for the eye and the working end. Cut it off, taking care not to cut any of the core fibers. Measure one short fid length from the working end and mark. Fan the tail and make an angled cut from the mark to the end to give a full taper to the core.

To taper the coat tail, begin at the R and count down five picks, or ridges, and mark. Continuing toward the working end, count off 15 picks and mark again. Cut the tail off square there. Unlay the coat back to the mark at the fifth pick, and make an angled cut from the fifth to the fifteenth pick.

Align the R and the two hash marks, causing the core strands to begin creeping into the coat. (Bunching usually prevents the strands from disappearing, but if they totally slip into the coat at this step, that's okay.)

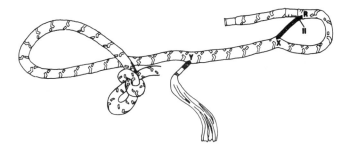

Tightly tape the tapered coat tail with masking tape; use as little tape as possible, but be sure to get all the loose ends. Smooth the coat from the slip knot down toward the eye; the core should slide back into the coat.

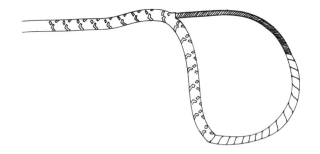

Attach the slip knot to a mounted hook, or have an assistant hold it. Smooth the coat over the core and coat-to-core joint. Begin gently, but if bunching occurs at the throat, roll and flex the area. If the coat does not move into position, use more muscle power and less finesse. You may have to pound on the rope with a wooden mallet to redistribute the strands.

Lock-stitch the splice into place (see page 44).

EIGHT

HOLLOW BRAID

Splices in hollow braid work on the same principle as the Chinese finger puzzle. After the working end is passed through the braid of the standing part and into the hollow of the rope, and the fid (see page 84) is removed, the strands of the braid return to their factory form. In doing so, they constrict, gripping the length of the rope tightly.

A special splicing tool, or fid, is made for this rope, but these fids are hard to find, so I recommend an alternative—a knitting needle with its endcap removed, or even a length of wire coat hanger. Either can be taped tightly to the rope while you work.

EYE SPLICE

TOOLS AND MATERIALS

Hollow-braid rope
Splicing tool (see chapter introduction)
Scissors or sharp knife
Marking pen

No exact measurements are needed to splice this rope, but for an eye or loop 3 inches (75 mm) or smaller, use the Locked Eye Splice described later in this chapter.

Lay out your rope and form the necessary loop. For splicing ropes of ¼ to ½ inch (6 to 12 mm) (the most commonly used sizes), allow about 1½ to 2 feet (450 to 600 mm) for the tail.

Taper the end of the rope by cutting it at a 45-degree angle. Pinch this tapered end into the hollow of the fid or slide it like a sleeve over the knitting needle or piece of coat hanger, then tape it tightly.

Insert the splicing tool through the braid at the throat of the splice. Ease the tip of the tool down through the hollow of the rope for a distance of 8 or 9 inches (200 to 230 mm), then poke it back out through the braid. Draw the tool completely out, pulling the tail through to adjust the eye to the desired size. Smooth the rope.

Pick up the tailpiece with the splicing tool attached and mark it where it exits the braid. Then pull on the tail until an additional 3 inches (75 mm) is showing, in effect shrinking the eye. Doubling the tailpiece back on itself, insert the tool at the mark on the tail and run it back down the tail hollow 2½ to 3 inches (63 to 75 mm) before pushing it back out through the braid.

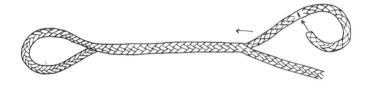

Pull the end through until the loop you have just formed in the tail disappears.

Cut the end close to the braid and push the cut strand ends back into the tail and out of sight.

Smooth the coat back into place.

Finally, work the tail back into the standing part so that the eye grows back into its proper size. As you go, note the unique property that causes this splice to hold: If you grasp the eye in one hand and hold the standing part of the rope in the other, the weave of the braid around the spliced section will tighten when you try to pull the tail back into the core, and the tail will refuse to budge. If you grasp the eye in one hand while pinching the braid opening in the throat of the splice with your other thumb and forefinger, you can easily pull the tail back through the braid until just its knobby end remains visible. Anyone who has ever played with a Chinese finger puzzle will understand why this works as it does.

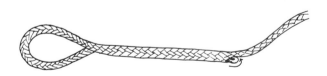

LOCKED EYE SPLICE

This is an easy and quick splice to execute. It is a good method to use if the eye is 3 inches (75 mm) or smaller.

TOOLS AND MATERIALS

Hollow-braid rope
Splicing tool (see chapter introduction)
Scissors or sharp knife

Lay out your rope and form the necessary eye. For rope of ¼ to ½ inch (6 to 12 mm) in diameter, allow about 10 inches (250 mm) for the tail. Taper the end of the rope by cutting the tip off at a 45-degree angle.

Push the tapered end into the hollow of the fid or affix it tightly to the splicing tool, as described for the previous splice.

Wrap the working end of the rope around the standing part to make a Half Hitch as shown in the drawing, and adjust the hitch until the eye is the desired size.

Insert the tip of the splicing tool into the standing part of the rope just above the hitch and ease the tool approximately 8 inches (200 mm) up through the standing part's core before poking back out through the braid. Pull the tool completely out and draw out the tail until snug.

Smooth the rope and cut the tail off close, tucking the cut strand ends back into the braid of the standing part until hidden from view.

END-TO-END SPLICE

Use this splice to join two ends of hollow-braid rope or to form an endless loop.

TOOLS AND MATERIALS

Hollow-braid rope
Splicing tool (see chapter introduction)
Scissors or sharp knife

Lay out the two ends of rope or, if you are making an endless loop, adjust to the correct size. For rope of ¼ to ½ inch (6 to 12 mm) in diameter, allow about 10 inches (250 mm) for each tail.

Taper both ends by cutting the tips off at a 45-degree angle.

Push one tapered end into the hollow of the fid or affix it tightly to the splicing tool, as described for the eye splice at the beginning of this chapter.

Measure 10 inches (250 mm) from the other working end and insert the splicing tool at this point, easing it up to the hollow core of the standing part for 10 inches.

Bring the tool back out through the braid, trim the end close, and tuck the strand ends back into the braid and out of sight.

Repeat for the other tail, inserting the splicing tool as shown in the drawing.

The splice will hold in use and is similar to the Chinese finger-puzzle principle described for the eye splice in this chapter.

NINE

COPOLYMER END-TO-END SPLICE

Because copolymer rope is still somewhat new to the market, its uses are still specialized. But this mix of polyethylene and polypropylene fibers is destined for increasing popularity. Copolymer is strong, easy to handle, economical, and resistant to stretching and shrinking, and it floats. Already it's replacing polypropylene as the rope of choice for New England's lobstermen.

So far, however, the rope is manufactured primarily in smaller diameters, and thus does not warrant eye splices. However, the Copolymer End-to-End Splice is useful for attaching two lengths together without a lumpy knot. And because of the construction of the rope (i.e., the core's two bundles of parallel strands contain the rope's strength, not the braided coat), we can't use a standard hollow-braid splice.

TOOLS AND MATERIALS

Rope

Splicing tool (there are no specialized tools for this rope, but
the copolymer splicing tool described in chapter 1 works well)

Scissors or sharp knife
Marking pen
Whipping twine and needle

Cut off the heat-sealed melted ends on the two ropes if necessary.

Measure back from both ends 14 inches (355 mm) and make
a mark on both ropes at that spot. At your mark, separate the
strands of the coat and then pry out the cores completely, back to
the ends.

Now, moving farther up the two standing parts, away from the
cut ends, make a second set of marks on the coats, another 14
inches (355 mm) beyond the first set.

Turn and adjust the two ends of the ropes so they face each
other.

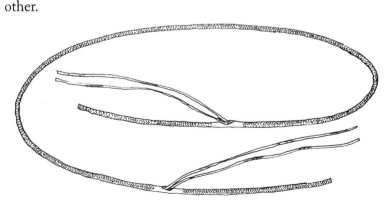

Insert the splicing tool into one of the ropes at the second mark (i.e., 28 inches/710 mm from the end). Run the tool down the center of the rope and poke just the tip out where the core exits the rope, at the first mark. Thread about 1 ½ inches (38 mm) of the end of the other rope's cover into the tip of the tool, then drag it back through and out at the second mark.

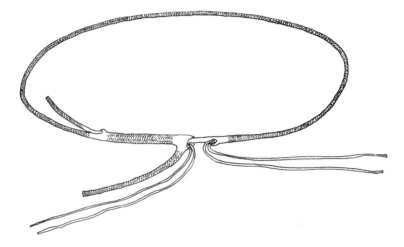

Turn the ropes and do the same to the other end.

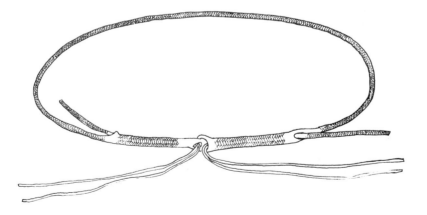

To splice in the two parallel cores, repeat what you did with the rope's covers.

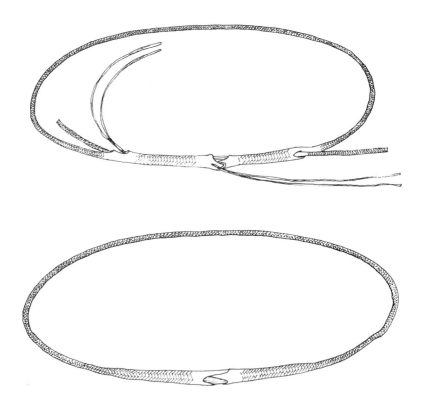

Milk out all the slack and bury the ends as shown, cutting and removing any core or cover tails.

Apply a tight whipping over the joint.

Due to the nature of this splice, some of the core will show at the marriage. You might wonder whether this splice has any real strength but, in fact, it does, due to the "Chinese finger-puzzle effect" described in chapter 8. Remember, too, that so far this splice has been used only with light-duty fishing gear, where it seems to work well. As this rope gains increasing acceptance, stronger, more sophisticated splicing techniques will evolve.

TEN

EIGHT-PLAIT ROPE

This rope is laid with eight strands that are worked in pairs for splice strength and appearance. Available in nylon, polyester, and Spectra, this is an inexpensive construction that resists twisting and hockling and, therefore, finds favor for commercial uses. I see a lot of eight-plait line on tugboats. Because the picks have a larger surface area for abrasion, however, it doesn't wear as well as double-braid.

If the manufacturer has not color-differentiated the two right-laid pairs from the two left-laid pairs, mark either pair with a pen to simplify the splicing process. (Directions are given with each splice for the length of rope to mark.)

EYE SPLICE

TOOLS AND MATERIALS

Eight-plait rope
Swedish fid
Vinyl tape
Scissors or sharp knife
Hot knife or heat source
Marking pen
Waxed whipping twine

Estimate the amount of rope you will need for the eye and mark either both right-laid strand pairs or both left-laid strand pairs for about twice this distance. Starting from the working end, count up the standing part of the rope 10 picks and seize the rope at that point with tape or twine.

Unlay the rope to the seizing, allowing the twist in the individual strands to remain. Tape the strand pairs together at their working ends.

Form the eye and take a painted pair of strands and tuck them at the throat under a handy unpainted pair in the standing part. A Swedish fid can make the process easier.

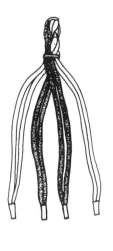

Turn the splice over and slip the other painted pair under the second unpainted pair. Always work so that you are tucking against the lay of the strands in the standing part. That is, if the standing pair twists from upper right to lower left, tuck under it from left to right.

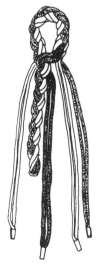

Turn your work a third time and tuck an unpainted strand pair under a painted pair. Turn again, and then tuck the second unpainted pair under the second painted pair. One round of tucks is now finished.

Complete *at least* two more rounds of tucks.

Cut off one strand from each pair 1 or 2 inches (25 to 50 mm) from the end. Tape or heat-seal the ends. Tuck the remaining single strands twice more, then cut and tape.

END-TO-END SPLICE

TOOLS AND MATERIALS

Eight-plait rope (2 pieces)
Swedish fid
Vinyl tape
Marking pen
Waxed whipping twine

Seize each rope tightly at the ninth or tenth pick. Mark both right-laid strand pairs or both left-laid strand pairs from the bitter end of each rope to about the sixteenth pick. Remove the tape or heat-sealed tips at the working ends, and unlay the strand pairs, leaving the twist in each strand. Tape the strand pairs at their ends, taking care that they do not become twisted together.

Align the ropes end to end. To marry the ropes, lace a painted pair of strands from the right-hand rope through the corresponding painted pair on the other rope, as shown in the illustration.

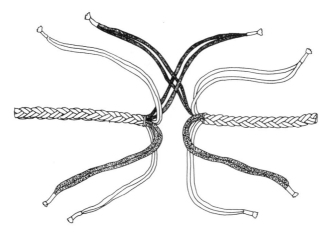

Lace the adjacent unpainted pair on the right-hand rope through the corresponding pair on the other rope.

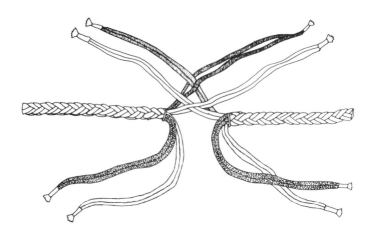

The other two strand pairs are laced in the opposite way: the painted pair on the left-hand rope is laced through the corresponding painted pair on the right-hand rope and, finally, the left-hand unpainted pair is laced through the last, opposite strand pair.

Draw the two rope ends together and seize with twine at the center to hold the developing splice in place. Remove the original seizings.

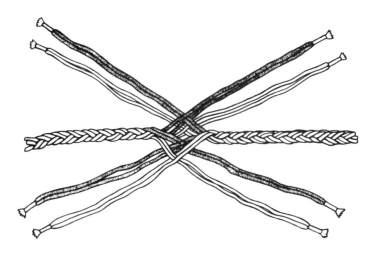

To begin the first round of tucks, insert one painted pair under the adjacent unpainted pair on the standing part of the mated rope and cinch tightly, then insert a pair of unpainted strands under the neighboring painted pair. Next, tuck the remaining painted pair and the remaining unpainted pair in the same manner, completing one round of tucks. Continue with additional tucks until 1½ inches (38 mm) of strands remain, and then repeat the procedure for the other side.

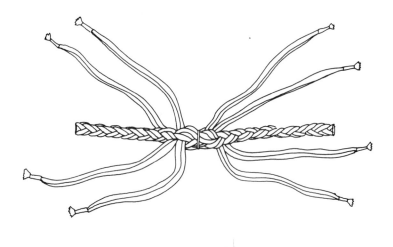

Cut off one strand from each pair. Tape or heat-seal the ends. Tuck the remaining single strands twice more, then cut and tape.

TEMPORARY EYE SPLICE

This Temporary Eye Splice is dependable and quick to execute. To be on the safe side, replace it with a standard eye splice at an early opportunity.

TOOLS AND MATERIALS

Eight-plait rope
Swedish fid
Vinyl tape
Scissors or sharp knife

Measure off 12 inches (300 mm) for the splice and, beginning there, form the eye. At the throat, with the point of the fid, separate the strands into clockwise and counterclockwise groups.

Reeve, or insert, the tail end through the opening by the fid. Move down three picks along the standing part from where the tail emerges, separate the strands in the same way as before, and reeve the tail back through in the opposite direction. Repeat this process twice.

Tape the tail to the standing part. The tail should be at least 3 inches (75 mm) long to allow for slippage.

ELEVEN

EIGHT-PLAIT ROPE-TO-CHAIN SPLICE

Technically, this splice belongs in chapter 10 on eight-plait rope, but it deserves a chapter of its own. This splice is superior to other systems for anchor rodes because there is no knobby shackle-and-thimble connection to drag across the deck. Also, it eliminates a shackle in a position where the pin often is lost from chafe or rust.

Chain is used on an anchor rode more for its weight than its strength. It lies on the bottom and helps to convert the force pulling on the anchor from vertical to horizontal so the anchor will be less likely to break out of the bottom and more likely to hold. Chain is also more resistant to chafing on rocks and coral heads. Match your chain to the anchor and shackle, as recommended by your supplier, and choose rope of sufficient diameter to be handled comfortably and to match the breaking strength of the chain. Be careful, however, not to buy rope so big that the strand pairs can't be laced through the chain links. Make sure the rope is nylon, which is elastic enough to function as a shock absorber when the boat bucks and tugs at its anchor.

ROPE-TO-CHAIN SPLICE

The Rope-to-Chain Splice and the construction of the eight-plait rope work very well together for anchor rodes, permitting the passage of rope and chain through a bow chock or hawsepipe. The eight-plait rope is excellent: Kinks and hockles fall right out, so it need not be coiled belowdecks. If eight-plait rope is not available, twelve-plait can be used instead; no shackle is needed. Be sure to work this splice up tight; excess slack in the spliced strands could cause abrasion.

TOOLS AND MATERIALS

Eight-plait rope
Chain
Sharp knife or scissors
Electrical friction tape
Serving mallet or reel-type serving tool
Whipping twine
Liquid rope seal (optional)

Measure the length of 12 links of chain to determine the required splice length for the rope. As an example, this distance is about 12 inches (300 mm) for $^3/_{16}$-inch (5 mm) chain. Pick up the eight-plait rope and measure the appropriate distance from the working end. Apply a good tight whipping (see chapter 13) at that point and unlay the rope back to the whipping. Notice the construction of the rope—four pairs of strands, each pair consisting of one strand of yarns twisted clockwise and one with yarns twisted counterclockwise.

Lay out the rope as shown.

Set the first link of chain directly on top of Strand Pair A and lace these two strands up through the link. Lace Strand Pair B down through the link, making sure it crosses Strand Pair A.

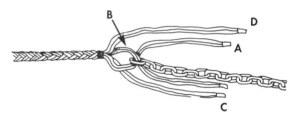

Repeat this procedure with Strand Pairs C and D through the second link, then return to Strand Pairs A and B for the third link, and so on. In this fashion, leapfrog down the chain. Two strand pairs cross through each link, and each pair skips a link before entering another from the side on which it exited in the previous pass.

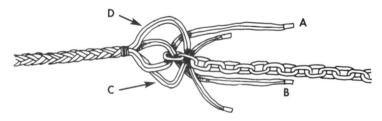

Continue this two-part process until ten links have been filled, then finish the splice on the eleventh and twelfth links. To finish, remove the tape from the strand-pair ends. Separate the two strands of each pair, pass one through a link (either the eleventh or the twelfth, as appropriate) and the other around the side of the same link. Then seize the two strands together closely, as shown, to prevent movement of the rope over the chain. Seal the strands by melting them with a match or hot knife. Applying a coat of liquid rope sealer would be a plus. As a final touch, serve the entire splice tightly with small stuff (see chapter 14) to further ensure that the strands do not chafe.

TWELVE

TWELVE-PLAIT ROPE

Constructed of nylon or polyester, this rope is used primarily on commercial boats for hawsers, docklines, and towlines. There is no need to coil twelve-plait; you can drop it in a heap and then just give it one or two good shakes to rid it of hockles and kinks.

EYE SPLICE

This splice can be completed with your fingers, but a fid will do a neater job.

TOOLS AND MATERIALS

Twelve-plait rope
Swedish fid (optional)
Vinyl tape
Scissors or sharp knife

The amount of rope necessary for this splice equals the circumference of the rope times seven (e.g., 1-inch/25 mm rope has a circumference of 3.14 inches/80 mm, so to make this splice in 1-inch/25 mm rope would require 22 inches/560 mm of rope). Determine this distance from the working end and tape the rope there. Unlay enough rope to be able to tape each of the 12 strand ends. Then unlay the rope to the tape, taking care to retain the individual twists.

Form the eye above the tape and mark the throat.

Group the strands into six pairs, each pair having one strand with its yarns twisting clockwise and an adjacent strand twisting counterclockwise. Tape the pairs together.

Divide the six strands into two groups, taking the three strand pairs on one side (to the left of the drawing) and reeving them directly through the middle of the rope at the mark on the throat. It is important to maintain the twist on the strands as they pass through the rope, and they must lay just right—not too loose or too tight. Snug the strands to remove excess slack.

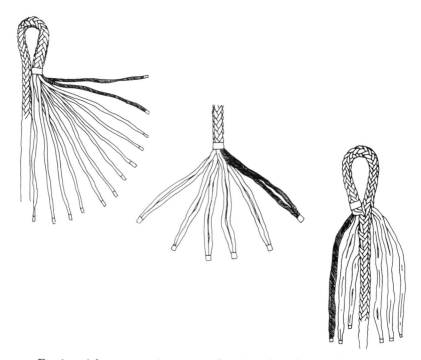

Begin with a convenient strand pair and tuck it under a nearby strand pair in the standing part of the rope.

Repeat with the five remaining pairs, making each tuck parallel with the one adjacent.

Complete two more rounds of tucks with each strand passing over one pair in the standing part before tucking under the next pair. Then begin tapering by trimming every other strand pair about 1 ½ inches (38 mm) from the standing part of the rope.

Complete another three rounds of tucks with the remaining strand pairs; then taper again, this time by cutting one strand from each pair. Retape the ends.

After another three rounds of tucks, draw up the three single strands tightly. Cut and tape their ends, leaving tails about 1 ½ inches (38 mm) long.

END-TO-END SPLICE

TOOLS AND MATERIALS

Twelve-plait rope
Swedish fid
Vinyl tape
Scissors or sharp knife

As in the twelve-plait eye splice, the amount of rope necessary for this splice equals the circumference of the rope times seven (for each rope). Determine this figure, and tape both ropes at that distance from the working ends. Unlay enough rope to be able to tape the 12 strand ends on each rope to prevent the yarns from raveling. Then unlay the ropes to the tape, taking care to retain the individual twist.

Group the strands into six pairs for each rope, each pair having one strand with yarns that twist clockwise and an adjacent strand with yarns that twist counterclockwise. Tape the ends of each pair of strands together.

To join, or marry, the two ropes, begin with any strand pair on one rope and lace it through the corresponding pair on the second. Lace the neighboring pair on the second rope through the corresponding pair on the first. Proceed in this way until all the strands are laced. Gently snug the two pieces together by drawing up the strands.

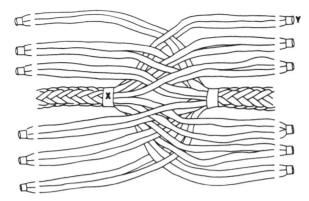

Distance from X to Y equals 7 times the rope circumference

To make the first round of tucks, pass any convenient strand pair over one nearby strand pair in the standing part of the other rope and draw it under the next two strands. Make parallel tucks with each subsequent strand pair to complete the first round.

Repeat with the second rope. Then complete two more rounds of tucks, working in the same way.

To begin tapering, trim off every other strand pair about 1½ inches (38 mm) from the standing part of the rope and tape the ends.

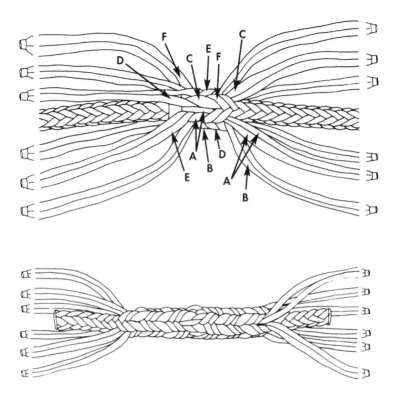

Complete another three rounds of tucks and taper again, this time by cutting one strand from each pair. Retape the ends.

Complete three more rounds of tucks with the three single strands. Then draw up the strand as you would a loose shoelace, until the pieces of the rope lay together but are not overly tight or loose.

Tape the ends, leaving a tail about 1 1/2 inches (38 mm) long.

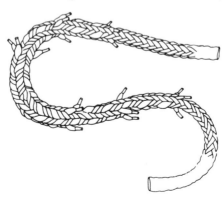

THIRTEEN

WHIPPING AND SEIZING

Both whipping and seizing are methods for binding rope, but whipping prevents the end of a rope from unlaying, while seizing binds two pieces of rope together, side by side. A traditional whipping is a tight winding of waxed or tarred small stuff; the more modern alternative is an application of one or two coats of a specially formulated liquid adhesive. Most marine supply stores carry these materials, often in kit form.

For seizing, many people now use plastic ties, which provide a quick, inexpensive way to bundle rope. Traditional seizing, however, looks good and will not damage or mark the rope.

TRADITIONAL WHIPPING

The width of the whipping should approximate the diameter of the rope. It is best to have two whippings a short distance apart—one near the rope end and one a few rope diameters farther up the standing part—with the small stuff pulled tight on each. If one is loosened, the other should keep the end from unlaying.

TOOLS AND MATERIALS

Rope to be whipped
Small stuff: waxed whipping twine
Scissors or sharp knife
Vinyl tape
Hot knife or heat source

Tape the end of the rope or, if it is synthetic, heat-seal the end with a hot knife or other heat source until the yarns are fused.

Begin whipping at least an inch (25 mm) from the bitter end of the rope. Lay a loop of small stuff across the rope, leaving a tail of 5 or 6 inches (125 to 150 mm) on the bitter end. You will need to grasp this tail later, so don't cover the tail completely with whipping.

With the working piece of small stuff, wrap around the rope from the tail end toward the apex of the loop, covering the loop until the width of the whipping is at least as wide as the diameter of the rope.

To end the whipping, insert the working end of the small stuff through the loop. Pull on the bitter end, or tail, of the small stuff until the loop slides completely out of sight. Clip the ends close.

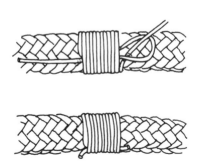

SAILMAKER'S WHIPPING

TOOLS AND MATERIALS

Rope to be whipped
Small stuff: waxed whipping twine
Sailmaker's needle

Take two stitches through the rope with the small stuff to secure its end. Then wrap the small stuff around the rope, working back over the stitches, until the width of the whipping approximates the diameter of the rope.

Draw the working end of the small stuff under the entire length of the whipping and pull it through.

Now bring the small stuff over the whipping (left to right in the illustration) to make the first angled stitch. Stitch through about one-third of the rope's girth, staying on the same side of the whipping.

Rotate the rope 120 degrees. Bring the small stuff back across the whipping to make another angled stitch—parallel with the first, but one-third of the rope's circumference removed. Stitch through the rope again, and make a third angled stitch. Continue in this fashion until all the stitches are doubled, then clip the end.

Note: For three-strand rope, the angled stitches follow the lay.

SEIZING

TOOLS AND MATERIALS

Ropes to be seized
Nylon small stuff

The size and construction of the small stuff are your choice.

Form a loop at the end of the small stuff and tuck the end two or three times through the lay of its standing part. If the ropes being seized are three-strand, work in the direction opposite the lay.

Circle the ropes to be seized, and anchor the working end of the small stuff by threading it through the loop and doubling it back upon itself. Apply eight to ten wraps around the ropes, taking care to cover the tail.

Take a hitch (as shown) and, working back across the seizing, place a layer of wraps over the first layer. These wraps are called *riding turns* because they "ride" on the first layer. The riding turns should not be as tight as the original turns and should number one fewer.

Pass the working end through the original loop and wrap two turns across the seizing, between the two ropes; take up any slack.

Tie a Flat Knot (see illustration). Draw the knot tight and clip close.

CHAFE PROTECTION

Somewhere along the line between the magnificent sailing vessels of the mid-1800s and today, chafing gear on ropes has disappeared. And that's a shame because today's ropes, with their high-tech fiber blends and state-of-the-art construction, demand protection for more reasons than the twisted manila, linen, and cotton rigging of old.

Good synthetic ropes are expensive, but they do not rot away. If you choose your ropes carefully and spend a little extra time applying chafing gear where needed, you should get years of useful service from them. I can assure you that you'll save both money and worry.

Lengths of garden hose or vinyl tubing are often used as chafing sleeves on mooring and anchor lines and sometimes in rigging, but the methods described here provide a more handsome alternative.

For the sake of simplicity, let us assume you are purchasing new ropes with plans to add chafing gear to the eye and/or at a point of probable wear on the standing part—that is, any place where the rope will repeatedly rub against a hard surface or another rope.

One type of chafe sleeve is fashioned from the coat of a double-braid rope. I like to use this for chafe protection on three-strand, hollow-braid, and plaited ropes. (For chafe protection on double-braid, I prefer to use leather, for reasons given later.)

Buy a short piece of double-braid the same diameter as your rope to make the chafe sleeve. There is no hard-and-fast rule on how long to make the sleeve. Decide how much length you'll need for the eye; then add 3 or 4 inches (75 to 100 mm) to allow for raveling at the ends of the sleeve and for the tendency of the sleeve to "collapse"—or shrink lengthwise—when you slide it over the rope you are protecting.

Remove the core from the double-braid and tape the resultant sleeve loosely at both ends. Then tightly and smoothly tape the rope end over which you will be sliding the sleeve. To make the job easier, sew one end of a cord to the rope end, making the cord a little longer than the sleeve.

Run the other end of the cord through the sleeve, then carefully remove the tape at the ends of the sleeve. (The sleeve ends will unravel for an inch or two/25 to 50 mm.)

With the ends free, the sleeve will expand enough to allow the rope to be pulled through. Use the cord to fish the rope through the sleeve.

Once the sleeve is on the rope, re-tape the sleeve just inside its raveled ends. Position the sleeve on what will be the eye. Trim the ends of the sleeve close to the tape and apply a few extra wraps to reinforce the ends.

Now splice the eye following the directions given in other chapters.

Double-Braid Coat as Chafe Sleeve

A leather chafe sleeve probably offers the best protection for both wire and fiber ropes, and I prefer this chafe protection for double-braid rope. Because there is a crossover step in the middle of the double-braid eye splice (see chapter 4), a sleeve would have to be applied in the middle of the splice; in all the confusion, it's easy to wind up with the sleeve either not on the rope at all or in the wrong place. The leather, on the other hand, can be wrapped and sewn after the eye is formed, and it looks better to boot.

Applying a leather sleeve can be complicated, but my instructions and a kit like the one manufactured by Sea-Dog (available from any marine store) will simplify the job. The kit will give you a piece of leather sized to the rope diameter you're covering, with holes prepunched along the mating edges. You also get needle, twine, and directions for sewing. (Unlike the chafe sleeve made out of double-braid, the leather sleeve is not moveable once it is applied, a fact that could be relevant when you're protecting a chafe-prone section of a standing part rather than an eye.)

Execute the double-braid eye splice almost to completion, stopping just short of the lock-stitch (see page 44). Mark the eye, then carefully "unmilk" the splice to expose the crossover. If the crossover is disturbed, the splice will be spoiled, so it is wise to stitch the crossover with needle and twine to prevent any slippage.

Unmilk the splice farther so that the marks on the core delineating the extent of the eye are in a straight line. Then put this straight-line section under tension with two lengths of small stuff, pulling in opposite directions. (Hitch the small stuff to the rope with timber hitches, as shown; see page 128 for a close-up view of the timber hitch.) A firm pull is all that is necessary. This will make the job easier because your hands will be free to hold the sleeve in place while you sew.

Keeping the seam to the outside of the eye and sewing as shown, wrap the leather sleeve according to the directions that come with the kit.

Release the rope and milk the splice back into place. It is not necessary to remove the stitches in the crossover.

Don't forget the last step, the lock-stitch (see page 44).

Leather Chafing Gear

You can, of course, use leather instead of a double-braid coat for chafe protection on twisted, plaited, and hollow-braid ropes

as well. Make marks on the rope where the eye is to be, then apply
the leather sleeve before you splice the eye. Put the marked section
under tension with two timber-hitched lengths of small stuff
pulling in opposite directions, thus freeing your hands to hold
and sew the leather in place. Arrange the leather's seam so it lies
on the outside of the eye. Release the rope from tension and complete the splice.

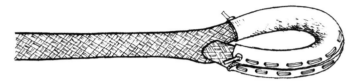

FOURTEEN

SEW-AND-SERVE EYE SPLICE

Served ropework lends an air of tradition and, for the owner of a traditional vessel, a few of these splices aboard would add a nice touch of the old days.

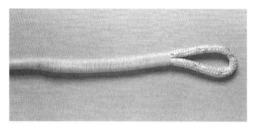

This splice works very well for double-braid, eight-plait, and twelve-plait rope. The splice requires a layer of serving; it is important that the sewing be very tight and the taper very smooth.

TOOLS AND MATERIALS

Double-braid rope
Serving mallet or heaver
Whipping twine
Sharp knife

Lay out your line forming the necessary eye. For the length of the splice, allow seven or eight times the inside diameter of the eye.

Place a tight seizing at the throat, then remove the tape or melted tip from the end of the tail and taper the tail smoothly with an angled cut through the coat and core. The cut should terminate 3 to 5 inches (75 to 125 mm) back from the end.

Comb, coax, and stroke the coat strands until they straighten along the axis of the tail. The strands will become indistinct, blending with the core yarns in the taper.

Then "marl" down the tapered tail by firmly binding it to the standing part with a series of hitches. Start at the base of the tail, passing the twine through the heart of the standing part and putting a stopper knot in the end of the twine. Work away from the eye, toward the end of the taper, tying off the other end in any convenient fashion.

Sew the two lengths of rope together between the marling and the seizing. Pass the needle and twine through the centers of both lengths of line by turns, pulling the twine as taut as possible as you go. Begin the stitching just below the throat seizing; when you reach the marling, start right back the other way, creating cross stitches as you go. Tie off the two ends at the throat with a square knot (see chapter 15).

marling

To set up the splice for serving, tie it up with a good strain, taut between two posts.

For serving, you'll need a serving tool, which dispenses small stuff in tighter turns than you can possibly achieve otherwise, or a serving mallet, the traditional alternative (see the heaver illustration in chapter 1).

Start the serving at the throat with twine and the mallet. After burying the end of the waxed twine beneath the first several turns, proceed with the serving until the entire splice is smoothly and tightly covered.

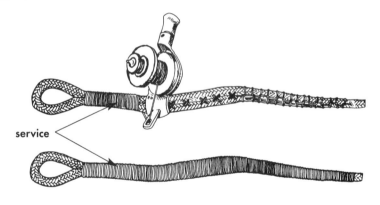

service

Allow only the last six or seven wraps to remain loose. Reeve the end of the twine back under the slack turns, snug the turns as tightly as possible, and cut the end close.

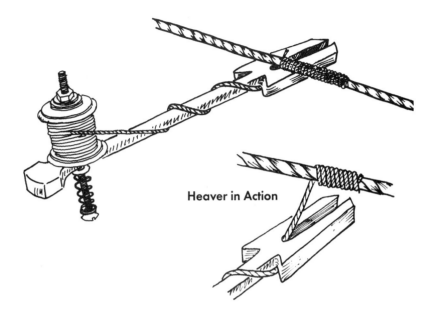

Heaver in Action

The design of an arborist style heaver or serving mallet is radically different from that of the sailor's standard serving mallet. At no time are any of the turns of the service out of sight because they are under the barrel of the standard mallet.

FIFTEEN

QUICK AND EASY KNOTS

Piecing together rope and placing eyes, or loops, at the end of rope require splices that offer a high degree of safety, strength, and dependability. The knots in this chapter, however, serve best in those light-duty situations not requiring the exceptional strength of a well-constructed splice. It is important to remember that the working load of a rope can be reduced by as much as half when it is knotted.

Among the 19 knots in this chapter are the 17 a sailor must master in order to become a licensed Able Bodied Seaman in the U.S. Merchant Marine (the outriders are the Package Knot and the Fisherman's Knot). In recent years, I've been teaching at the New England Maritime Institute, one of a handful of such schools that appeared around the country in the wake of the *Exxon Valdez* disaster. Consistency and safety are the prime directives. The U.S. Coast Guard requires each licensed mariner to know these knots by heart.

The first pair of knots belong to the group known as *stopper knots* because their function is to stop a rope from slipping through a block, clutch, or other hardware. The simplest stopper knot is the lowly but useful Overhand Knot. Add another twist and you get the bulkier and therefore more useful Figure-Eight Knot.

Overhand Knot

Figure Eight

Hitches are used to secure the end of a line to an object, either to move the object or to belay the line and keep it from moving. The Clove Hitch is a versatile, quick-to-tie choice for light and temporary duty, but the Rolling Hitch provides an added measure of security. The Stopper Hitch is especially effective for a super grip—say, when towing a timber through the water or dragging it across land.

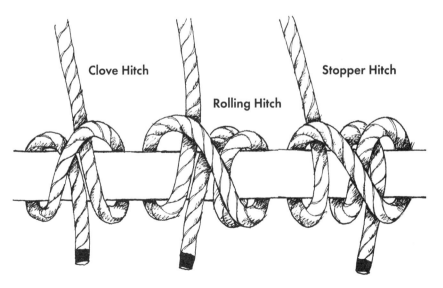

Clove Hitch   **Rolling Hitch**   **Stopper Hitch**

If the stopper hitch fails you, try the Timber Hitch, a great choice for picking up a long, round timber or spar. But if it's a bucket or barrel you're lifting, you won't find a simpler, more effective knot than the Barrel Hitch finished off with a Bowline (see below).

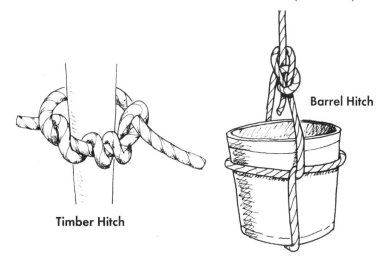

Barrel Hitch

Timber Hitch

Returning from the exotic to the mainstream, the Two Round Turns with Two Half Hitches has a self-explanatory name if there ever was one. This is a good, secure belay for the end of any line. And let's not forget the Anchor Bend, which, despite its name, is really another hitch. Tie it through the ring of your anchor and rest easy, especially if you take the trouble to seize the end to the standing part.

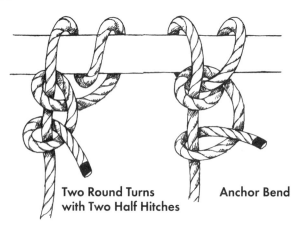

**Two Round Turns
with Two Half Hitches**

Anchor Bend

Bowline

A mariner finds many needs for a loop in the end of a line, to slip over something or to tie around something. Docklines, tow-lines, painters, lashing lines—many is the line that spends some portion of its working life sporting a loop in one or both ends. For a permanent loop, nothing beats an Eye Splice, but for a temporary loop, the Bowline (above) is a workhorse of a knot. There are many methods for tying it—all of them easy—and it's just as easy to untie. A Bowline on a Bight (below) is a good choice when you require two loops that will be subjected to approximately equal ten-sion in the same direction. It works well as a bosun's chair.

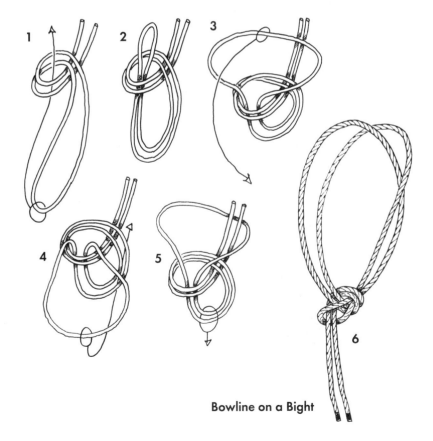

Bowline on a Bight

The French Bowline, properly tied, produces an excellent rescue sling. The two loops adjust automatically to the parts of the body they encircle. The Running Bowline produces a slip knot that is relatively easy to untie. To tie it in a heavy dockline or hawser, one end of which is already belayed, make the small loop (i.e., the "rabbit's hole"), then "frame" the knot with a big loop, as shown. Pass the end under the beginning of the big loop, then back up through the small loop, behind the standing part; then down through the small loop again as for an ordinary bowline. Now, when you pull a bight of the standing part up through the big loop, you'll have your slip-knotted loop to drop over a bitt or bollard (1).

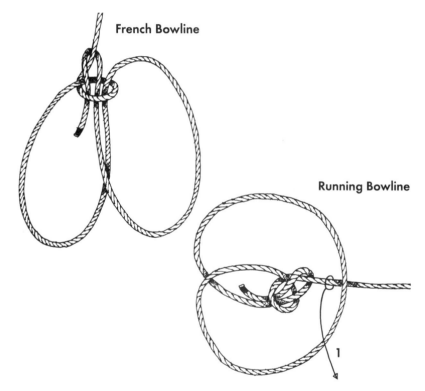

French Bowline

Running Bowline

1

The Cat's Paw is a simple but elegant knot designed to reduce the chances of a heavy load slipping off the hook of a block and tackle. Twist the loops as shown into the sling holding the cargo, then drop the loops over the hook. It won't jam, and it will spill instantly when removed from the hook.

Cat's Paw

A bend is called for when the time comes to tie two ends of rope together. The most common bend, although not the best, is the Square Knot, or Reef Knot. A square knot should not slip if it is tied with two ends of the same size, but it can lock under tension, making it difficult to untie. The square knot usually should not be used to join two pieces of rope except as a temporary expedient because it is not particularly secure and will capsize easily if rubbed the wrong way by, say, a shroud or bobstay. It's the knot of choice for tying reef points under the bunt of a reefed sail—thus, the alternate name. Tied wrong, this knot becomes a Granny Knot and is more likely to slip.

Square Knot

The Package Knot is simply a square knot with an extra turn in the first overhand. It is a good alternative to the square knot because it is easier to untie. It does not hold as well, however.

Package Knot

The Fisherman's Knot is strong and easy to tie, but untying it is very difficult. (In the illustration, the knot has not yet been cinched tight.)

Fisherman's Knot

The Sheet Bend is much easier to untie than a square knot after it has been under strain, and is an excellent choice to join ropes of different sizes. When a ship is docking, for example, the smaller line is thrown onto the ship from the dock and is then tied with a single (or double) sheet bend onto the ship's dockline (often wire). Then the dockline is hauled over to the dock and belayed. When one of the lines already has an eye in it, the knot is called a Becket Bend. It is important to pull the knot tight so the loops seat firmly with *like* ends parallel to each other. If this bend is not drawn tight properly, the two pieces can slip.

Sheet Bend

Towing hawsers can be joined with a Carrick Bend. If the ends are not seized onto the standing part of the rope, however, the knot can seize under strain and be difficult to untie.

Carrick Bend

SIXTEEN

LIVERPOOL WIRE SPLICE

The instructions here are for a basic 7 × 19 "soft-eye" splice that can be used as a lizard (which works like a bungee cord) for a temporary fairlead. The ³/₈-inch-diameter (9 mm) 7 × 19 is easy to work with; if you haven't made this splice before, use galvanized wire, which is less springy than stainless steel. Stick to a soft-eye splice (no thimble) until you get the hang of this wire splice: a thimble makes the eye harder to keep in the vise.

The splice is shown here with a tight service through the whole eye area. This protects you by preventing the individual strands from shifting and popping the eye out of the vise while you're making the splice, and it ultimately protects the wire from weather and early wear. The strands of a wire bent into a curve become compressed or flattened on the outside edge of the curve. This distortion causes the wire to lose strength. Service corsets the wire, holding it to its rounder shape and protecting the splice and eye from moisture.

TOOLS AND MATERIALS

Your 6-foot (1.8 m) length of ⅜ inch (9 mm) 7 × 19 wire
"Parrot-beak"-style and diagonal wire cutters
Rigging vise and marlinspike
Tarred tape or friction tape
Pine tar or some water-repelling mixture
40 feet (12 m) of tarred twine or marlin
Sharp knife
Marking pen
Vinyl tape
Safety glasses

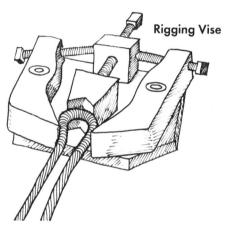

Rigging Vise

Pictured here is a small rigging vise. Made by Mr. Z (available at auctions, marine flea markets, and marine antique stores), it's bronze and measures 4 × 5 inches (100 × 125 mm). It's adjustable three ways by turning the screws. For fine-tuning or tightening, it's a good idea to have a wrench close by. The rigging vise's only purpose is to aid splicing stranded wire in sizes from the smallest to ⅜ inch (9 mm).

Here's how to start. On your length of wire, mark a spot 2 feet (600 mm) up from the working end (mark 1, next page). From that spot, apply pine tar or water-repellent coating toward the working end for a distance of about 7 inches (175 mm). Working back toward mark 1, wrap a layer of tarred tape over the tar. Then wrap the service, which becomes your eye, working from mark 1 toward the working end, against the lay of the wire.

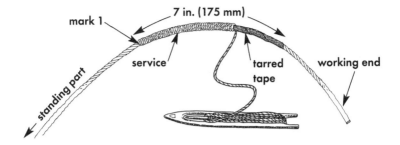

Clamp your wire in the vise the "right way," literally. To do this, stand facing the vise with the wire bent in your hand. The working end of the wire—the 2-foot (600 mm) end—should be in your right hand; the standing part should be in your left. Now put your piece in the vise and clamp it down. During splicing, you'll probably want to stand on the left side of your work.

On the working end, unlay all the strands and tape the ends.

Insert the marlinspike into the wire at the marked point from left to right, as shown below (mark 1). Take care to go over the top of the heart, or core, of the standing part and pick up only three strands of the standing part. Now rotate the marlinspike one full circle down the wire around the heart of the standing part, as if the spike were a sort of propeller with the wire as its hub. The spike will travel down the wire from position 1 to position 3. Leave the marlinspike stuck through the wire.

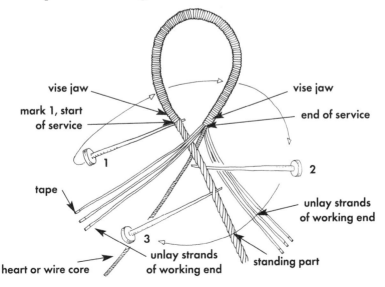

Put on safety glasses and bring Strand 1, the innermost strand of the working part (the one that nearly "kisses" mark 1) into position so it lies on top of the standing part at mark 1. Then bring Strand 1 completely under the standing part and make a gentle turn in the strand so you can tuck it back through the space made by the marlinspike, right to left, at position 3.

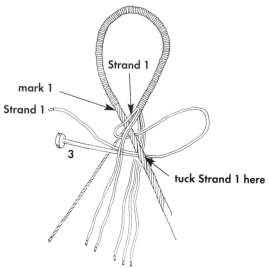

Roll the spike back from position 3 to the start of the service (mark 1), position 1, and simultaneously gently pull back the slack out of the wire.

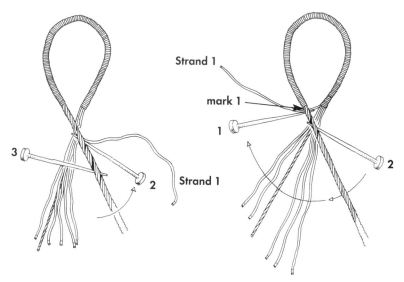

Insert the marlinspike over the heart at mark 1 and pick up only two strands of the standing part this time. Rotate the marlinspike as before so it travels down the wire. Insert Strand 2 (the strand next to Strand 1) of the working end at the same place as Strand 1, but exit the standing part one strand farther away from the beginning of the service (mark 1). Roll the spike back, close to mark 1. With Strand 3, pick up only one strand. Remember to have it enter at the same spot as Strands 1 and 2.

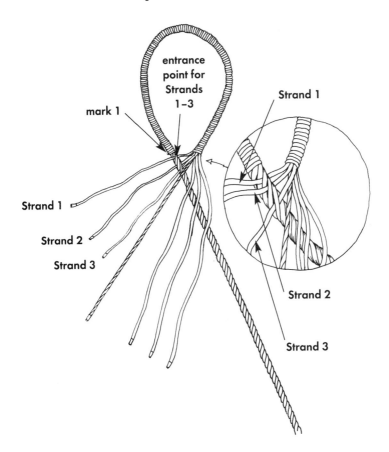

To hold your work in place, use the marlinspike to tuck Strand 3 five more times. As you rotate the marlinspike down the wire, wind the working strand around the wire *with* the lay, always tucking Strand 3 under the same working strand.

Now we have to bury the heart of the working end. Insert the marlinspike in the same spot where Strand 3 was first tucked, and set the heart across the wire and behind the spike (A). This motion or method is different from tucking. For lack of a better description, we're going to pry the heart of the working end into the center around the heart of the standing end for several inches. You'll get the knack pretty quickly because the wire will bind your tool if you're doing it the wrong way. Another thing: if your work is looking a lot different from the examples, don't be so quick to blame yourself; there is a ton of poor-quality wire for sale these days. Bury the heart of the working end for about 18 inches (450 mm) and tape it so it can't spring out.

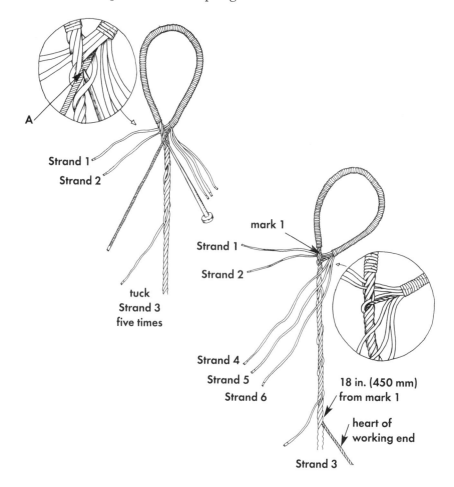

A

Strand 1
Strand 2

tuck
Strand 3
five times

mark 1
Strand 1
Strand 2

Strand 4
Strand 5
Strand 6

18 in. (450 mm)
from mark 1

heart of
working end

Strand 3

To tuck Strand 4, put the spike in the same space into which the heart went, picking up just one strand. Tuck Strand 4 six times. Pick up the next strand down (Strand 5) and tuck it six times. Finally, using the next strand down on the standing part of the wire, do the same with Strand 6. Now go back to the beginning and tuck Strands 1 and 2 each about five more times. It'll be hard to keep track of how many tucks you've made on an individual strand, but don't worry about it. It makes a better splice if the strands exit at different points, which creates a tapered splice. Clip off the wire tails close with the diagonal cutters.

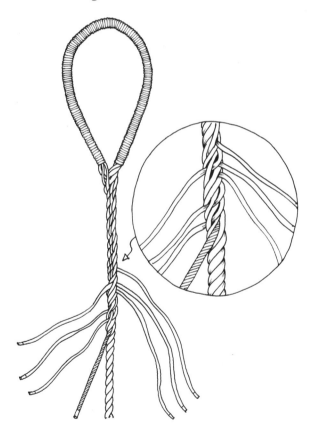

Apply your service as described earlier in this chapter, starting at the base of the splice and working up to the eye. Now remove the finished and serviced splice from the rigging vise.

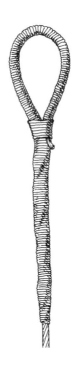

SEVENTEEN

MAKING YOUR OWN ROPE

Rope designers use methods such as the following when working with a new fiber or yarn to get a feel for how much material is needed to make a specific rope and how much it will need to be twisted during manufacture. Many thousands of feet of rope have been sold from displays of short samples made this way.

TOOLS AND MATERIALS

Twine (at least 10 feet/3 m)
Scissors or sharp knife
Wooden pencil
Vinyl tape

If you are using nylon twine, tape the ends to prevent unlaying. Tie one end of the twine to a fixed hook. Holding the pencil horizontally about 3 feet (0.9 m) from the hook, alternately pass the twine around the pencil and hook until you have made at least $1\frac{1}{2}$ complete rounds, the equivalent of three rope yarns. The diameter of the twine and the number of rope yarns formed will determine the diameter of the strand of rope you are making. This strand will be one-half the diameter of the finished three-strand rope, although you will triple your worked piece after the initial twisting.

When you have three or more yarns, tie off the unsecured end to the pencil or hook. Pull on the pencil to impose a uniform tension and length on the yarns.

Lightly grasp the bundle of yarns in the fist of your left hand with the pencil resting outside your thumb and forefinger. The tube formed by your fist is similar to a ropemaker's strand tube.

While keeping tension on the bundle of rope yarns with your fist, turn the pencil clockwise with the index finger of your right hand to form the rope strand. The number of twists you put into the strand will determine the firmness of the finished rope. You should stop twisting before the rope kinks; if it does kink, just turn the pencil counterclockwise until the kink disappears.

Grasp the pencil with your right hand and keep tension on the strand throughout this step. With two fingers of your left hand, grasp the strand midway between the pencil and the hook, forming a bight. Pass the pencil behind the hook and back again, inserting it through the bight of strand in your left hand. Don't let the strand go slack.

You now have three parallel and highly twisted strands. Grasp them with a fist as before, and twist the pencil counterclockwise until it stops. The finished rope won't unlay of its own accord. Ropemakers refer to this characteristic as *balance*.

Tape the rope just shy of each end and cut off the ends. You now should have a short piece of three-strand rope that looks as though it was cut as a sample from a large spool of machine-made rope.

GLOSSARY

anchor cable—Chain, line, wire, or a combination of them used to attach a vessel to its anchor.

belay—To secure a rope with turns around a cleat or bit.

bend—Knot used to join two ropes.

bight—A loop in a length of chain or rope.

bitt—Wood or iron post on a deck for securing mooring lines or towlines.

bitter end—The nonworking end of a line or chain.

bollard—Iron mooring post on a pier.

breaking strength—Load required to break a rope under tension during a prescribed test.

chafe—To wear or fray a rope.

clew—The lower after corner of a fore and aft sail

coat—The outer covering of two-part rope.

coil—Neat circles of rope, line, or chain piled to keep the loops free of tangles.

cordage—Rope or rope-like material varying in size from twine to hawser; in nautical handiwork, rope of less than ¹/₂ inch (12 mm) diameter, or small stuff.

core—The inner section of two-part rope.

diameter—Measurement of cross section of rope through the center. For noncritical use, determine by measuring rope's circumference, or girth, and divide by 3.

eye—A spliced loop in a rope.

fake—A circular pile of rope; it is organized and on one plane. A Flemish coil.

fid—A splicing tool used to guide the rope strand into place.

halyard—Any rope or wire used to hoist sails.

hardness—A measure of the force required to open the strand of a rope. A hard rope almost stands by itself.

hawsepipe—Metal tube that allows passage of the anchor cable to the chain locker.

hawser—Towline or mooring line more than 5 inches (13 cm) in circumference.

heart—The center strand or core of a wire rope, of layed wire, or lubricated wire.

heaver—A handmade tool used to apply service.

hitch—Knot used to tie a line to a hook, ring, or spar.

hockle—A condition whereby a rope strand twists on itself. Also called a chinkle.

jury rig—Make or fix using ingenuity and whatever materials are at hand.

kink—A tight hockle that upsets the lay of a rope.

knot—A weak substitute for a splice, but easy to unfasten.

lanyard—A length of small stuff, sometimes decorative, tied to an object to make it secure.

lash—To secure with rope.

lay—The direction of the twist in a rope strand (see right-laid).

line—Rope with a specific use.

make fast—To secure a rope.

marl—A form of seizing.

marline—Two-strand, left-laid, tarred hemp.

marlinspike—Steel tool used to separate strands in a wire rope during splicing.

marry—To interlace two ropes, end to end, for splicing.

mooring lines—Rope used to tie a boat to a wharf or pier.

mousing—Seizing used to prevent a pin from unscrewing and falling out of the shackle or to close the opening of a hook.

pick—On the surface of a braided rope, the visible yarn between the emergence from and the exit to the inside of the braided rope.

picks per inch (ppi)—The number of parallel picks in 1 inch (2.5 cm) of braided rope. The picks per inch, selected at manufacture, determine strength and flexibility of the braided rope.

preventer—A length of wire chain or line that acts as a safeguard or backup tether to keep an object (e.g., a boom) from moving unexpectedly.

reeve—To pass the end of a rope through a hole.

right-laid—Rope with strands twisted up and to the right when the end points away from the viewer.

serving—A smooth covering on line or wire.

serving mallet—Hammer-like tool used to apply wrapping turns around a line or splice.

small stuff—Rope of less than ½ inch (12 mm) diameter.

splice—Careful entwining of rope components.

standing part—The area in the rope that is inactive, as opposed to the working end, bitter end, or bight.

surge—Let the strain off a line intermittently, in a controlled fashion.

tackle—A system of lines and blocks to gain additional lifting or pulling power.

take a turn—Run a line around a cleat or bitts.

taper—To diminish the diameter of a rope smoothly by selectively removing strands or yarns.

thimble—A grooved ring made of plastic or metal that fits tightly inside an eye splice.

tuck—To push a single strand through the body of a rope (fiber or wire).

twine—Rope of a diameter larger than a sewing thread but smaller than a shoelace.

unlay—To take the twist out of a three-strand rope. The ends of the three strands are taped to prevent them from unlaying.

vang—A tackle positioned on the vessel to prevent the boom from raising.

whip—Wrap the end of rope with small stuff to prevent the rope from unlaying.

working load—A manufacturer's recommendation of the maximum pounds of pull to which a rope can safely be subjected; generally, one-tenth the new rope's breaking strength.

working part—The end of the rope you are using to make a splice (compare with standing part).

yarn—A group of fibers twisted together; thread.

INDEX